D1085797

Property of
Charles A. Owen Jr.
Medieval Studies Library

Xavier Barral i Altet

Series Editor: Henri Stierlin
Photos: Claude Huber, Anne and Henri Stierlin

THE ROMANESQUE

Towns, Cathedrals and Monasteries

TASCHEN

Köln Lisboa London New York Paris Tokyo

Front Cover

Cross-section of the choir of the abbey church of Cluny III, 1089–1130 (see page 118)

Page 3

The survival of the Triumphal Column
Column of Christ, Hildesheim cathedral, originally made for the church of Sankt Michael, circa 1015–1020. 3.79 m high and 0.58 m in diameter, this monument to the greater glory of Christ is inspired by the triumphal columns of the Roman Emperors Trajan and Marcus Aurelius. Trajan's column showed the Emperor's victories over the barbarians; here the scenes display Christ's triumph over death and evil. The quality of the work testifies to the standards of metal casting attained by the Ottonian craftsmen.

Page 5

Aquarius, the water-carrier
This relief from Tournai cathedral shows a woman pouring water out of a vessel. It dates from the twelfth century and is part of a series of sculpted representations of the signs of the Zodiac, which occur frequently in portal sculpture.

About the author:
Xavier Barral i Altet is Professor of Medieval Art History at the University of Rennes. A highly regarded expert on the Middle Ages, he is a former Director of the Museu d'Art de Catalunya, has contributed to a number of fundamental works on the Romanesque, such as *Le monde roman 1060–1220*, 2 vols., Paris, 1982–1983, and *Le Paysage monumental de la France autour de l'an mil*, Paris, 1987, and has published many articles in specialist journals.

About the editor:
Henri Stierlin was born in Alexandria in 1928, and after Classical Studies worked as a journalist and produced numerous radio and television programmes on the history of civilisation. From 1964 to 1972 he worked as editor on the 16-volume standard work *Architecture Universelle*.

© 2001 Taschen GmbH
Hohenzollernring 53, D-50672 Köln
www.taschen.com

Editor-in-chief: Angelika Taschen, Cologne
Edited by Caroline Keller, Cologne
Co-edited by Karl Georg Cadenbach, Düren
Design and layout: Marion Hauff, Milan
English translation: Chris Miller, Oxford
Cover: Catinka Keul, Cologne

Printed in Italy
ISBN 3-8228-1237-4

Contents

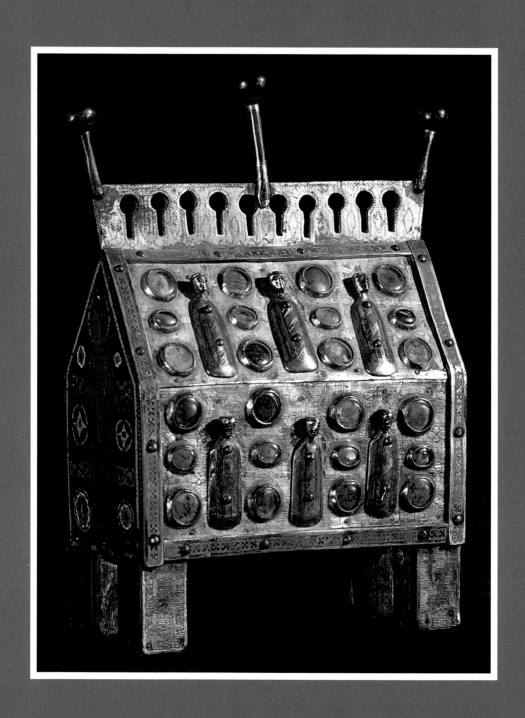

INTRODUCTION

Art and History

The Romanesque treasures of the Iberian Peninsula
Reliquaries, vases and other liturgical objects make up the treasure of a church. The intricately worked gold and silver and the motifs on this reliquary (dating from the twelfth century) display superlative craftsmanship. The Romanesque goldsmiths of Navarre, Castile, León, Asturias and Galicia were celebrated throughout Europe. (Museu Nacional d'Art de Catalunya, Barcelona)

In 987, Hugues Capet came to the throne of France, and the Capetian dynasty succeeded that of the Carolingians. The eleventh century saw the feudal system develop, with its division of society into peasants, knights and clerics. By its end, royal power had been reduced to its lowest ebb by powerful and quarrelsome neighbours, above all the dukes of Normandy, now also kings of England. The realm was confined to the Île de France. In the early twelfth century, Capetian power was reasserted by Louis VI the Fat (reigned 1108–1137); aided by Abbot Suger, the instigator of the Gothic style, he enforced order in the unruly royal domain. The centres of feudal power were losing ground to the increasingly populous towns, where trade brought together artisans, merchants and the developing middle class.

The Crusaders captured Jerusalem in 1099, in 1122 the Investiture Contest was settled, in 1130 Roger II was crowned King of Sicily, and in 1138 the advent of the Hohenstaufen dynasty to the Imperial throne marked the beginning of the conflict between Guelphs and Ghibellines. In 1152 Frederick I Barbarossa became German Emperor; in 1154 the Plantagenet dynasty came to the throne of England. Finally, in 1214 Philippe II Auguste (reigned 1180–1223) defeated the Emperor and the Count of Flanders at Bouvines, and in so doing brought down the coalition organised by the English king, John. Richard I, the Lionheart came to the English throne in 1189, reigning for ten years. Frederick II of the Hohenstaufen dynasty reigned as King of Sicily (1198), of Germany (1217), and as Emperor of the Holy Roman Empire (1220–1250). The Fourth Crusade captured Constantinople in 1204.

Though the art of the Middle Ages bears the traces of these events, European artistic development was far from uniform. Romanesque art continued to flourish in southern France, the Iberian Peninsula and Italy during the late twelfth century; in northern France, the Gothic had first appeared in the 1140s. Thus the Romanesque Pórtico de la Gloria at Santiago de Compostela, the façades of the abbey church of Santa Maria at Ripoll in Catalonia, and the great churches of northern Italy are considerably later than the façade of Chartres with its Gothic sculpture.

Only when this duality is acknowledged can one grasp the monumental art of the late twelfth and early thirteenth centuries as a whole. The art of the Renaissance presents a similar duality. It developed in Italy in the late fourteenth century; elsewhere in Europe, Gothic prevailed throughout the fifteenth century, as the diffusion of Flemish altarpieces testifies. This raises important questions about the circulation of artistic models, the spread of influence and the relation of styles.

Our understanding of Romanesque architecture dates from the mid-nineteenth century, when the term was invented to define the period of medieval architecture preceding the Gothic; since the style was thought to derive from Roman architecture, it was called 'Romanesque'. (In England the style is often referred to as 'Norman'.) In religious architecture, Romanesque art is characterised by the sculpture with which interiors and exteriors were decorated, especially in the twelfth century. Religious sculpture constituted an offering to God, and in it we discover the perfect expression of the doctrines, aspirations and purpose of Romanesque art.

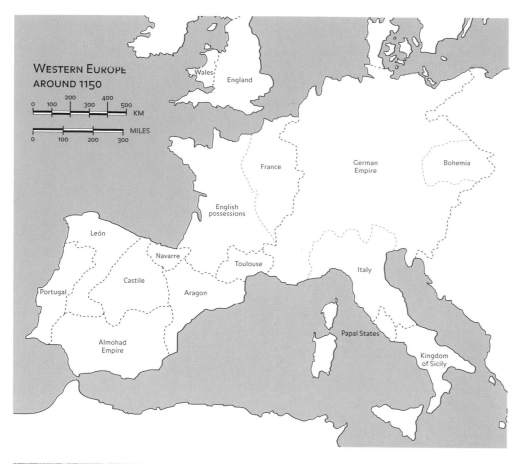

WESTERN EUROPE
AROUND 1150

Medieval cosmic imagery
Linen cloth and embroidery,
92 x 97.5 cm, late tenth century.
This hanging from the relic shrine
of two holy brothers, both named
Ewald, shows the personification
of the year, Annus, in the centre
of two concentric circles, holding
Day and Night in his hands. In the
inner circle are the four elements,
in the outer the twelve signs of
the Zodiac. This cosmic vision
rests on Sea and Earth (below) and
is integrated into God's order by
Alpha and Omega (above). (Relic
chamber, Sankt Kunibert,
Cologne)

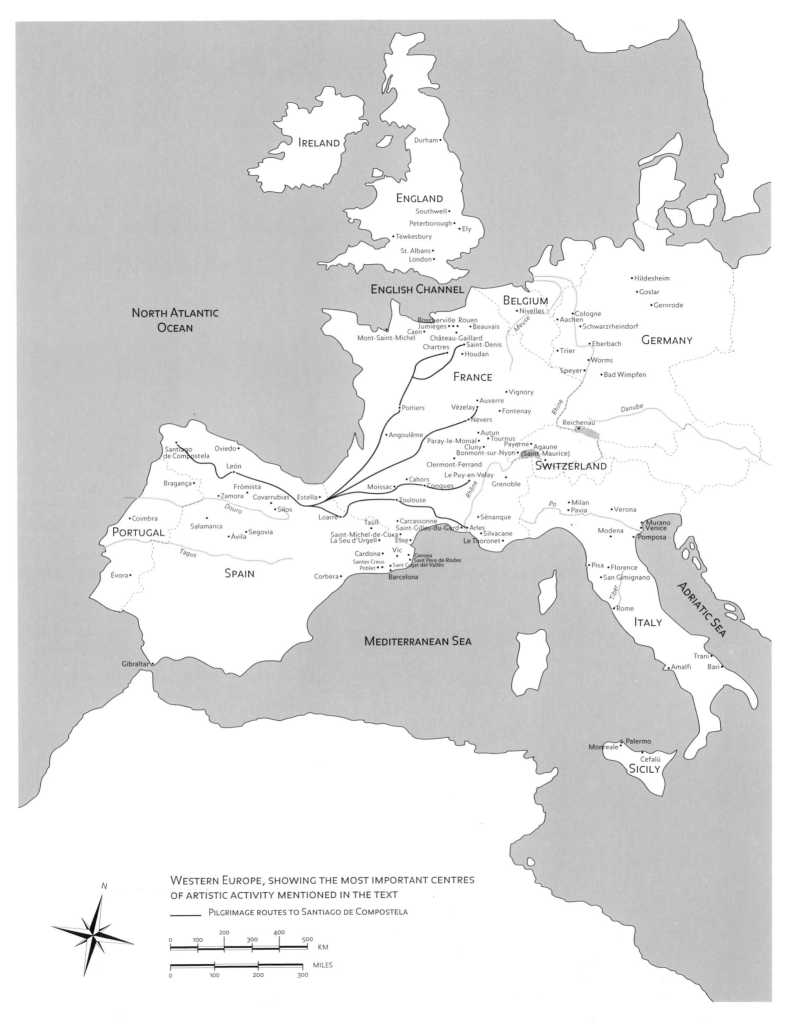

IRELAND

ENGLAND
Durham •
Southwell •
Peterborough • • Ely
• Tewkesbury
St. Albans •
London •

ENGLISH CHANNEL

NORTH ATLANTIC
OCEAN

BELGIUM
• Nivelles

GERMANY
• Hildesheim
• Goslar
• Gernrode
Cologne •
Aachen •
Schwarzrheindorf •
Meuse
Boscherville Rouen
Jumièges • • • • Beauvais
Caen •
Mont-Saint-Michel
Château-Gaillard
Chartres • Saint-Denis
• Houdan
• Eberbach
Trier •
Worms •
Speyer • • Bad Wimpfen

FRANCE
• Vignory
• Auxerre
Vézelay • • Fontenay
Rhine
Danube
Poitiers •
• Nevers
Reichenau
• Angoulême
Autun
Paray-le-Monial • • Tournus
Cluny
Bonmont-sur-Nyon • Agaune
(Saint-Maurice)
Clermont-Ferrand •
Santiago
de Compostela
Oviedo •
León •
Le Puy-en-Velay •
Grenoble •
SWITZERLAND

Bragança •
Frómista •
Zamora •
Covarrubias •
Estella •
• Silos
Moissac • • Cahors
Conques •
Po
• Milan
Verona •
Douro
• Toulouse
Loarre •
Sénanque •
Pavia •
Coimbra •
Taüll •
Carcassonne •
Saint-Gilles-du-Gard •
Arles •
Silvacane •
Modena •
Murano
Venice
PORTUGAL
Salamanca •
Segovia
• Ávila
Saint-Michel-de-Cuxa •
La Seu d'Urgell •
Elne •
Le Thoronet •
Pomposa
• Vic
Pisa •
Florence •
San Gimignano •
Tagus
Cardona •
Gerona •
Santes Creus • Sant Pere de Rodes
Poblet • Sant Cugat del Vallès
Tiber
Évora •
SPAIN
Corbera •
Barcelona
ITALY
• Rome

Gibraltar •

MEDITERRANEAN SEA

ADRIATIC SEA

Trani •
• Amalfi
Bari •

Palermo
Monreale •
Cefalú •

SICILY

N

WESTERN EUROPE, SHOWING THE MOST IMPORTANT CENTRES
OF ARTISTIC ACTIVITY MENTIONED IN THE TEXT

—— PILGRIMAGE ROUTES TO SANTIAGO DE COMPOSTELA

0   100   200   300   400   500
KM

0   100   200   300
MILES

The Emergence of New Forms

The Creation of the Romanesque

Page 11
Christ Triumphant at Sant Climent, Taüll
A detail of the painted decoration of the semi-dome of the apse, circa 1123. This very stylised head of Christ is a summation of Romanesque art. Its intensity demonstrates the yearning expressed by Romanesque artists for the return of the risen Christ. (Museu Nacional d'Art de Catalunya, Barcelona)

An Ottanian antependium
This gold antependium (120 x 175 cm) made from gold, silver-gilt, jewels and cabochons was presented to Basle cathedral by Henry II and his wife Kunigunde. It dates from around 1019/1020, and scholars dispute whether it originates from Fulda or from the Reichenau. Christ is shown holding a globe and blessing between arcades, with the donors at his feet, flanked by the Archangels Michael, Gabriel and Raphael and Saint Benedict. This is a chief work of Ottonian art. (Musée du Moyen Âge – Cluny, Paris)

Pre-Romanesque

Many changes occurred around the first millennium. Among these was the emergence of a new style of architecture, the pre-Romanesque, which prepared the transition between Carolingian and Romanesque architecture. Since civic art is known to us only through archaeology, religious architecture affords the finest examples of the monumental art of this period. Numerous donations combined with the religious ardour of the builders to clothe the West in new churches. They were erected to replace those that had been destroyed during the barbarian invasions of the Roman Empire and later of northern and western Europe, and they were built in stone rather than wood. Their greater size was commensurate with the increasing numbers of Christians and the increasing size of monastic communities. They constituted a rich display of architectural novelty intended to impress the people, honour the divine, and offer a shelter worthy of the precious relics that they housed. The creations of the millennial period, though they relied on classical, Byzantine and Carolingian tradition, constituted a highly original artistic achievement.

In the tenth century, Italy was the scene of a number of architectural innovations. One of these was the crypt, which raised the floor-level of the choir. In the second half of the tenth century the ambulatory was introduced in Ravenna and Verona. The formula of a choir flanked by towers was introduced at Aosta and Ivrea. Even though Rome remained faithful to the paleo-Christian tradition, as illustrated by the church of San Bartolomeo all'Isola, built by Otto II on a basilican plan, northern Italy was already showing the characteristics of the first southern Romanesque by the tenth century; the style spread to southern France and Catalonia some fifty years later.

In France, remarkable monuments were constructed during this period, such as the old cathedral at Reims, rebuilt by Adalbéron around 976, or the foundations established in Orléans by Robert the Pious, which we know about thanks to the early eleventh-century account of Helgaut, a monk from the monastery of Fleury. Later reconstruction has at least partly destroyed a large number of the major churches of the tenth century, such as the old cathedral at Chartres, built by Fulbert, Saint-Aignan at Orléans, and, in southern France, Saint-Victor at Marseilles and the great abbeys of the south-west. What remains of this period is principally towers and crypts. The most common form of crypt comprises a single room, with rounded walls reflecting the curve of the apse, divided into nave and aisles by columns and capitals carrying groin vaults. The rotunda of Saint-Bénigne at Dijon in Burgundy perfectly illustrates the model of superposed upper and lower crypts. At the abbey church of Saint-Aignan in Orléans the crypt contains a *confessio*; in Saint-Avit, in the same town, it functions as a second nave. At Clermont-Ferrand, apses and little chapels prefigure the formula of ambulatory with radiating chapels. The ambulatory-and-radiating-chapel formula perfected in Saint-Martin at Tours was to become one of the principal glories of the pilgrimage churches of the eleventh and twelfth centuries.

A new wall structure
Notre-Dame-de-la-Basse-Œuvre, Beauvais, late tenth century, west façade. The façade is pierced by a portal and a large window. The small, cubic stones – Roman *spolia* – are set in abundant mortar. A single clover-leafed cross set in the gable and a frieze running over the head of the window are the only decorative elements in this very sturdy ensemble, which prefigures the monumentality of the later Romanesque façades.

Page 15
Traditional solidity
Notre-Dame, Jumièges, about 1040–1067, west end. The façade of the abbey church presents a porch; the tribune is reached via staircases in the lateral towers, which are 46 m high. Each has a sturdy base, two storeys of blind arcades, and two octagonal storeys, the latter of which have suffered considerable alterations. The overall effect perfectly illustrates the Romanesque harmonic façade.

Traces of the great monuments built in this period have survived. First and foremost was the abbey church of Cluny II (963–981), which pioneered the echelon apse scheme. The nave and side-aisles were extended by a rather narrow transept with a tower at the crossing. Around 1000–1010 a narthex was constructed at the west end. This comprised an entrance crypt with upper sanctuary, framed by two towers. This new formula played an important role in the evolution of architecture during the second half of the eleventh century. The church of Saint-Vorles at Châtillon-sur-Seine reflects the Cluniac model very accurately.

In the Oise, Notre-Dame-de-la-Basse-Œuvre at Beauvais provides, despite certain lacunae and numerous restorations, important testimony about tenth century

A clerestory passage
Notre-Dame, Jumièges, 1040–1067, crossing. All that remains of the two-storey lantern tower at the crossing is the west side, which still reaches its original height of 41 m. A clerestory passage runs in front of the windows and connects it with the tower, an arrangement characteristic of Anglo-Norman buildings.

architecture. Its plan follows the Carolingian model: nave and aisles, preceded by an imposing porch and extending into three apses, are supported by bays carried on supports quadrangular on the north and octagonal on the south side. The very simple elevation exhibits high windows placed on the axes of the arcades, which light the nave and aisles; the whole is completed by a transept with crossing tower and flat east end.

In Normandy, the abbey of Notre-Dame (begun 1040) at Jumièges has, alas, survived only as a ruin. But what is known of it also displays the characteristics of its period. The nave attained a height of 25 m, and nave and aisles were divided into four bays by piers with engaged semi-columns. It had a three-storey elevation, with large arcades, tribune and clerestory. The nave roof was of timber, while the side-aisles and tribunes were groin-vaulted between transverse arches. The projecting arms of the transept were divided into two bays and carried tribunes. A lantern tower stood at the crossing. The structure of the west end comprised a porch and two superposed tribune galleries, flanked by two tall square towers. Their lower portions form an imposing base for the four further storeys. The two lower storeys are adorned with blind arcades; the upper two merge into the octagon. As the first one of its kind in Normandy, this two-tower façade built in 1045 illustrates one of the essential steps in the evolution away from the Carolingian west-end structure towards the more harmonious Romanesque façade.

The church of Saint-Étienne at Vignory in Champagne, consecrated in 1050, suggests a transition towards the Romanesque ambulatory. It has a central nave and side-aisles with timber roof leading to a very wide choir with aisles; the latter is

A tribune gallery
The three-storey elevation of Notre-Dame at Jumièges (circa 1040–1067) comprises arcades with semicircular double-moulded arches, tribunes opening on to triple-arcaded bays, and a clerestory composed of widely splayed windows without ornament. This triple elevation provides an emphatic verticality in the nave walls.

divided into two bays by powerful pillars, which were perhaps originally intended to carry a bell-tower. The chevet was built between 1051 and 1057, and comprises a sort of protoambulatory with three radiating chapels. This design arose from the need for circulation around either the relics placed beneath the main altar or those in the radiating chapels. The decoration too prefigures the later Romanesque characteristic of architectural sculpture. Above the great arcades of the nave are false tribunes with bays opening on to the aisles. These are divided by short colonnettes carrying capitals whose geometric decoration foreshadows the earliest Romanesque. This is also true of the sculpted decoration of the imposts placed above the pillars, at the springing line of the arcades. And the capitals on the pillars of the apse, which alternate with square piers, are decorated with face-to-face or back-to-back quadrupeds wearing a very Romanesque air.

In the Île-de-France, the abbey church of Saint-Germain-des-Prés played an important role in the spread of early Romanesque sculpture and of the porch bell-tower.

The architecture of southern Europe prior to the tenth century continues the tradition of late antiquity. The paleo-Christian basilicas continued to be used throughout the High Middle Ages. A good example of the chronological stages of this style can be found in the group of episcopal buildings at Terrassa in Catalonia. The chevets of Santa Maria and Sant Pere (San Pedro) exhibit carefully laid courses of small ashlared stones, which are sometimes attributed to Visigothic masons (sixth to seventh centuries), but seem more likely to be ninth-century. Sant Miquel (San Miguel), which was later used as a baptistery, is central in plan and presents the

A chevet with ambulatory
Saint-Étienne, Vignory, consecrated 1050, chevet. The bell-
tower rises over the north aisle
of the choir. A second bell-tower
faces it from the south aisle,
though only the lower storey was
ever constructed. The ambulatory
features three radiating semicircular chapels. The effect is
somewhat austere, as the wall-
surfaces are animated only by
small window-openings, but from
this design the Romanesque
echelon apse was to develop.

same kind of masonry. This group also affords information about the place of episcopal groups in southern towns; it gives us some idea of the previous appearance of
similar groups at La Seu d'Urgell and Vic in Catalonia.

The tenth-century architecture of the Mediterranean coast is known to us primarily through small buildings, most of which are of rectangular plan. They often,
though not invariably, lack aisles and are generally timber-roofed. Apses are normally small and roofed with half-dome or semicircular vaults, the earliest being of
horseshoe plan inside and square or polygonal outside; the horseshoe shape is later
found inside and out, and this evolved into the characteristic semicircular shape of
the Romanesque apse. This development is first encountered in lateral apsidioles,
as at Sant Quirze at Pedret, and reaches full definition in the main apses, as at Saint-
Génis-des-Fontaines and Saint-André-de-Sorède. Nevertheless, throughout the

Above left

An early Romanesque capital
Saint-Étienne, Vignory, consecrated 1050, capital from the open
tribune. Above the nave arcade
open a series of bays divided by
short colonnettes with sculpted
capitals. The neck of the capital is
decorated with two registers of
stylised foliage. In this ornamentation we recognise the first
timid steps towards Romanesque
decorative carving.

Above right

The Romanesque bestiary
Saint-Étienne, Vignory, capital
in the apse. The columns in the
choir of the apse are crowned
with capitals whose flat surfaces
are carved with animals. These
stylised lions and quadrupeds,
some of them addorsed, already
wear a distinctly Romanesque air.
The stylistic contrast between
these capitals and those of
the nave reveals how rapidly
Romanesque ornamental sculpture developed.

False tribunes
Saint-Étienne, Vignory, interior
of the nave. Between the arcade
and the clerestory is a sort of open
tribune arcade giving directly on
to the side-aisles. This arrangement is thought to be a reminis-
cence of classical antiquity, and
is rarely found.

tenth century, rectangular and trapezoidal apses predominated. The transept may
be higher than the nave, as at Sant Pere at Terrassa or Canapost, or lower, as at Saint-
Génis-des-Fontaines. Sculpture remains essentially architectural, and the capitals
are reused classical ones or derivatives of Corinthian.

The most coherent building of the second half of the tenth century is the former
Benedictine abbey church of Saint-Michel-de-Cuxa in the Pyrénées-Orientales. Its
nave is twice as wide as the aisles, and is divided into three bays by rectangular pillars and arcades. The transept is low, and projects widely from the body of the
church; its north end has been demolished. The chevet presents a rectangular central apse, typical of tenth-century architecture, but which has been completed by
four lateral semicircular apses, which foreshadows the advent of Romanesque.
Originally there was a door opening on to the exterior on either side of the central

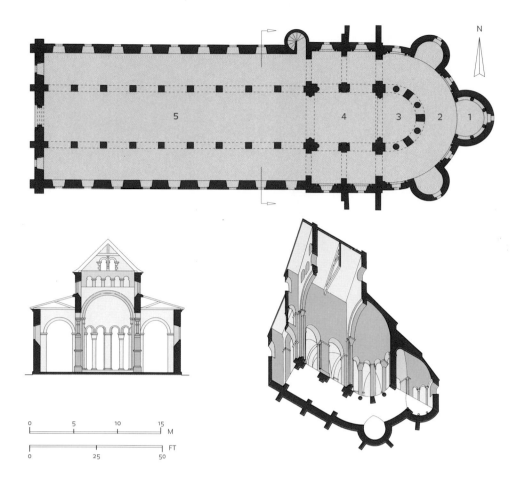

An influential plan
Saint-Étienne, Vignory, consecrated 1050, plan, cross-section
of the chevet and isometric projection. The nave (**5**) is flanked by
single aisles and opens directly on
to the chevet; the transept does
not project. The chevet comprises
two bays of aisles (**4**) with buttressing intended to support a
crossing tower that was never
built. The ambulatory (**2**) around
the choir (**3**) leads to three radiating chapels (**1**) and its inner edge
is a semicircular arcade in which
square pillars alternate with
columns. Saint-Étienne marked a
significant step in the development of the ambulatory.

apse. The nave is timber-roofed and lit by embrasured windows. All this is highly characteristic of the tenth century, as are the irregular masonry of the walls,
covered in mortar, and the much larger stones used at the corners. But Saint-Michel
is known above all for the horseshoe arches of its arcades, in which the piers project
beyond the imposts. The arches are constructed with staggered voussoirs in the
lower part of the arch and radiating stones in the higher part, and pertain not to
Islamic tradition but to a local and classical one.

Saint-Michel-de-Cuxa is an excellent source of information about large-scale
pre-Romanesque architecture and the many buildings that have not survived, such
as the cathedral of Vic, the church of Santa Maria at Ripoll, and the cathedral at La
Seu d'Urgell. In Roussillon, this last phase of Catalan pre-Romanesque has left
traces in the three-apse chevet and wide transepts found at Saint-Génis-des-
Fontaines and Saint-André-de-Sorède. Traces of Catalan pre-Romanesque also survive in the Languedoc regions closest to Catalonia, such as Hérault and Aude. The
abbey church of Saint-Michel-de-Cuxa is vital to our understanding of the transition
between pre-Romanesque and the first southern Romanesque.

Page 21
Carolingian influences
The nave and aisles of Saint-
Étienne at Vignory carry a
wooden roof. The diaphragm
wall that divides the nave from
the choir is pierced with two
registers of windows, nineteenth-
century alterations. The aesthetic
ideal governing Saint-Étienne
remains pre-Romanesque.

Late tenth-century architecture in the Pyrenees

Saint-Michel-de-Cuxa, plan of the abbey church, second half of the tenth century. The nave and aisles open through horseshoe arcades on to projecting transepts. Each of these has two deep contiguous apsidiole chapels, with barrel vaults inclining slightly to the horseshoe. The rectangular apse is typical of tenth-century architecture.

1 Nave
2 Transept
3 Apsidiole chapels of transept
4 Apse

Local tradition in Saint-Michel-de-Cuxa

The nave opens on to the aisles through three arcades, the lower part of which, constructed of large stones, supports the irregular masonry above. The famous horseshoe arches spring from imposts outside the line of the pier. Modified in the sixteenth century, they derive from a local tradition.

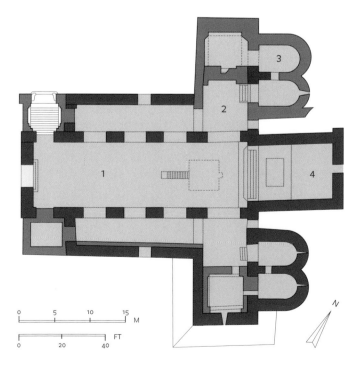

Transitional architecture
Saint-Michel-de-Cuxa, second
half of the tenth century. Across
the cloister lies the entrance to
the abbey church, whose structure
dates from the tenth century. The
bell-tower, sole survivor of the
pair flanking the transepts, is
eleventh-century. The masonry
of the walls and the splayed
windows distinguish the pre-
Romanesque from the eleventh-
century sections. The cloister is
twelfth-century.

The First Southern Romanesque

The earliest Romanesque appeared in the south. A distinctive form of religious building spread rapidly from southern Italy through southern Gaul (Provence) to Catalonia. The masonry comprises small stones roughly shaped with the hammer and laid in fairly regular courses to imitate brickwork. These buildings generally adopt a classical basilican plan with or without side-aisles (Ripoll, Cardona, Tournus) but there are also central-plan buildings derived from late antiquity. A transept is sometimes found, though it is generally low and its arms truncated. The first stone coverings were barrel vaults with continuous semicircular arches, lacking transverse arches and inspired by Roman models. Later, the nave tended to be barrel-vaulted with transverse arches, and the side-aisles to be groin-vaulted.

The church of Saint-Martin-du-Canigou (consecrated in 1009) in the eastern Pyrenees was one of the first buildings to be entirely vaulted. The superposed higher and lower churches share the same plan: three barrel-vaulted spaces leading to an apse. The problems of balance created by placing one vaulted structure on top of another forced an alteration of the initial plan. The three east bays on both levels are supported by small monolithic granite columns; thereafter solid masonry surrounds the columns of the basement and the arches are reinforced. In the western bays of the lower church, powerful cruciform pillars were used, and the three barrel

Left

The prestige of the bell-tower
Pomposa, Benedictine abbey of Santa Maria, façade and bell-tower, twelfth century. A very simple porch comprising three arches is richly decorated with tiling, terracotta, stone carving and openwork. The number of openings in the tall rectangular tower is proportioned to the height. This type of Romanesque bell-tower, which served to express the prestige of the religious community, proved very popular in northern Italy, at Fruttuaria, Milan, Como and Ivrea.

Lombard bands: a new form of ornamentation
Pomposa, Santa Maria, detail of the decoration of the bell-tower, eleventh century. The wall is covered with blind arcades and vertical bands. These bands project very slightly from the wall, and are connected at the top by little arches. The number of arches is variable. This motif is found on the façades, chevets and bell-towers of first southern Romanesque and was still used in the twelfth century.

A distinctive chevet
Sant Ponç, Corbera, late eleventh century. The nave and aisles open on to a rectangular crossing, with a dome on a square base. The apsidal chapel and two apsidioles are semi-circular. All this is characteristic of the first southern Romanesque. Original here is the staircase across the roof of the chevet.

Sober elegance
Sant Ponç, Corbera, detail of the external wall. The external walls of the aisles and transepts are decorated with pilaster strips separated by two blind arches, a form of decoration characteristic of the first southern Romanesque.

Blind niches
Sant Vicenç, Cardona, 1040, view
from the crossing into the choir.
It displays extreme austerity of
decoration. Blind niches animate
the internal walls. This decorative
motif is Roman in origin.

An early masterpiece
Sant Vicenç, Cardona, isometric
projection and plan. A porch with
tribunes precedes the nave, which
has three bays and a semicircular
barrel vault on transverse ribs. The
aisles are groin-vaulted. The walls
are reinforced inside by pilasters
with offsets and outside by buttresses. The transept projects only
slightly; the crossing carries a
dome on squinches. The choir
has one orthogonal bay.

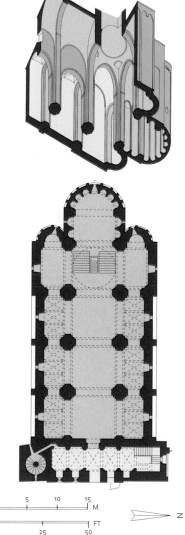

vaults were reinforced by transverse arches; in the upper church the monolithic
columns and continuous barrel vault were used throughout.

These exercises in vaulting from the first manifestation of Romanesque were
confined to relatively small-scale buildings. The appearance of transverse arches
meant that piers tended to become cruciform and to be reinforced by engaged
columns and offsets. Piers were also used to support the bays of the great arcades,
which came to define the rhythms of internal spaces. The arcaded bay made possible the articulated architecture that continued in use throughout the Middle
Ages. Walls were very thick; the few windows were narrow. The apse was raised on
a crypt. The crypt was normally a low room, slightly below ground level, whose
vaults were carried by columns; its plan and horizontal dimensions were those of the
apse. The crypts of the first Romanesque period were perfectly suited to the
increasingly popular cult of relics. Crypts rarely extended beneath the full width of
the crossing. The crypt of Saint-Martin-du-Canigou, replicating the dimensions of
the upper church, was exceptional.

Another very distinctive trait of this architecture is the octagonal tower, generally built at the crossing, where it rose above a dome carried on squinches. Bell-
towers were often added; they were usually placed at the chevet or the façade, and

Page 27
A jewel of the first southern Romanesque
Sant Vicenç, Cardona, 1040, chevet. The spacious choir is raised over the semicircular apse. The walls are ornamented with Lombard bands, and little niches underline the cornices of the chevet. The church is part of a fortress that was thoroughly restored in the 1960s. Its technical and artistic perfection make this one of the masterpieces of first southern Romanesque.

A powerful bell-tower
Square in plan, the bell-tower stands on the right of the former abbey church of Sant Pere de Rodes, dating from the twelfth century. It has plain window openings in its lower section, and double windows and oculi in its upper part. The walls are decorated with Lombard bands. The impressive proportions and the ornamentation of the bell-tower are directly inspired by the first southern Romanesque.

were generally square. The number of openings in the successive registers of bays generally increased with the height of the tower. This formula is very common in Italy. The west façade of Santa Maria at Pomposa (Emilia) presents a porch and a campanile dating from the mid-eleventh century. The campanile has no fewer than nine registers defined by decorative pilaster strips (see below). The lower storeys have one opening, the top two have four.

Buildings from the first half of the eleventh century sometimes lacked sculpted decoration, and in these the architects created an original decoration by varying the masonry of the walls. The internal walls were decorated with large niches similar to those in the mausoleums and bath complexes of Roman times, and the baptisteries and *martyria* of the early Christian era. The architecture of the first Romanesque period often exhibits a decoration of blind arcades and so-called 'Lombard bands'. These are vertical bands placed high up on a wall beneath the cornice and ornamented with little arches framed by slender pilaster strips. Between the two pilaster strips there may be two, three, four or more arches. Lombard bands are

A highly original elevation
Sant Pere de Rodes, consecrated in 1022. To help carry the transverse ribs of the semicircular barrel vault in the nave, the supports have been given a high pedestal, which projects laterally and into the nave. From these pedestals rise the columns of the arcades, and the two superposed columns with remarkable sculpted capitals that support the transverse ribs of the nave.

often found on apses and the outer walls of naves; they mark the storeys of bell-towers, and delineate the structure of façades.

The distinctive traits of the earliest, southern, Romanesque attain great technical and artistic perfection in the collegiate church of Sant Vicenç (San Vicente) at Cardona in Catalonia. Consecrated in 1040, it has a wide, lofty nave, with a semicircular barrel vault supported by transverse arches and massive pillars with dosserets. The dimensions of the three bays of the nave are based on that of the crossing, which is covered with a low dome, pierced with narrow openings and carried on squinches. From the outside, this defines a centre governing the volumes of the chevet and the transepts. The building is extremely austere; its external decoration is confined to Lombard bands and blind niches underlining the cornices of the choir. The bands recur on the internal walls of the chevet and apse. Another Catalan building, the monastery of Sant Pere de Rodes (San Pedro de Roda), is ambitious and innovative in plan; it possesses a rudimentary ambulatory without radiating chapels, intended to facilitate circulation. By this time the cult of relics had gained considerable significance in religious life. The church, consecrated in 1022, is a large building with a two-storey elevation; it is nevertheless vaulted throughout.

The influence of the first southern Romanesque is also to be observed a little later in the monastery of San Martín at Frómista in Castile-León. Here the nave and aisles lead to three apses in echelon scheme. The masonry is of small stones. At the crossing a dome on squinches is surmounted by an octagonal tower. The façade is framed by two cylindrical turrets, which derive from the Carolingian heritage. The rich decoration of the capitals and modillions is a forerunner of the great Romanesque achievements in monumental sculpture.

A continued adherence to the first southern Romanesque style is a distinctive feature of Catalan Romanesque. The churches of Santa Maria and Sant Climent (San Clemente) at Taüll were consecrated in 1123. They retain many of the characteristics of early eleventh-century buildings: small-scale masonry, pilaster-strip decoration and tall, slender bell-towers. Subsequently, the quality of masonry underwent a slow but steady improvement. Innovations originated for the most part in northern Italy. The cathedral of Santa Maria at La Seu d'Urgell, begun before 1131, thus presents a chevet with a high arcaded gallery; the archives associate this with the name of an Italian architect. It is a feature found in many Romanesque buildings in the Po Valley. Examples include the cathedral at Modena, San Michele at Pavia, Santa Maria Maggiore in Bergamo and Santi Maria e Donato at Murano.

An early carved capital
The nave of Sant Pere de Rodes boasts exceptional guilloche- and leaf capitals from the eleventh century. Their style marks the transition from early medieval to Romanesque art.

Page 31 above
The first southern Romanesque in Catalonia
Sant Climent, Taüll, consecrated in 1123. The church is basilican in plan. The masonry is made up of small stones roughly trimmed by hammer. The windows are few and narrow. The slender bell-tower is square in section; it stands alongside the choir. Its many windows and rich decoration of Lombard bands enhance its elegant proportions. It reveals the fidelity of the Catalan tradition to the formulas of the first southern Romanesque.

Early monumental sculpture
Saint-Génis-des-Fontaines, Pyrénées-Orientales, lintel of western portal, 1019–1020. In the centre Christ sits in a double mandorla borne by two angels; he is flanked on either side by three apostles beneath arcades. The horseshoe arches of the arcades and the dry, angular representation of the drapery suggest Hispanic influence. The composition is perfectly suited to its architectural setting, and suggestive of the origins of Romanesque sculpture.

Page 31 below
Architectural sobriety
Sant Climent, Taüll, plan and isometric projection (left, centre) and Santa Maria in the same town (right). The church of Sant Climent has nave and side-aisles with a pitched roof carried on the rectangular imposts of the masonry columns. The nave opens directly on to a central apse and two apsidioles. This arrangement is also found at Santa Maria, Taüll, which was, however, much altered in the eighteenth century, when the nave vault and lantern tower were constructed.

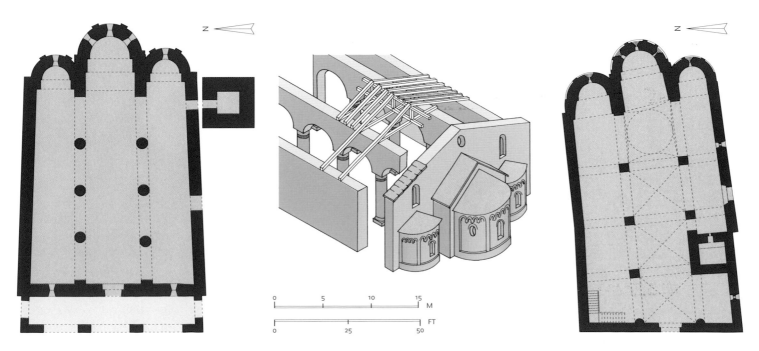

Monumental apse painting
Sant Climent, Taüll, consecrated 1123, mural painted on the semi-dome of the apse. The painting illustrates the triumphal return of the Messiah at the end of time. Above the apostles Christ appears in majesty within a mandorla, his feet resting on a hemisphere representing the earth. He is surrounded by the four Evangelists carrying their symbols. The expressive faces and wealth of colour make this one of the masterpieces of Romanesque painting. (Museu Nacional d'Art de Catalunya, Barcelona)

Burgundian mural decoration
Saint-Philibert, Tournus, eleventh century, detail of the south wall of the south tower. The wall is lit by windows with semicircular arches framed by colonnettes. A remarkable decoration composed of bands of blind arcades and of chevrons covers all the walls, showing how far to the north the use of such ornament had spread. The loopholes of the lower storeys add to the impression of formidable power.

The abbey church of Saint-Philibert at Tournus testifies to the extent of southern influences in Burgundy; this is true of both architecture and mural decoration. The building is preceded by an imposing narthex derived from the Carolingian two-storey westwork, but the decoration of Lombard bands and blind arcades is typical of the first southern Romanesque. The narthex is three bays long, vaulted and divided into nave and aisles by cylindrical masonry piers crowned by simple imposts. The church itself possesses nave and aisles separated by two rows of piers similar to those of the porch, but carried to a greater height. The transverse barrel vaults of the nave transfer the thrust on to the diaphragm arches of the nave walls and thus make a clerestory possible. For the first time direct lighting thus became possible without the thrust of the vault forcing the side walls out of true. The chevet stands above the crypt and is extended by a large apse with ambulatory, off

The westwork adapted
Saint-Philibert, Tournus, west façade. Before the main church rises an imposing westwork on the Carolingian model of the two-storey narthex. Originally, two stubby towers stood over this massive base, but in the second half of the twelfth century a bell-tower with many window openings was added to the north tower. The overall effect is transitional between the Carolingian westwork and the Romanesque harmonic façade.

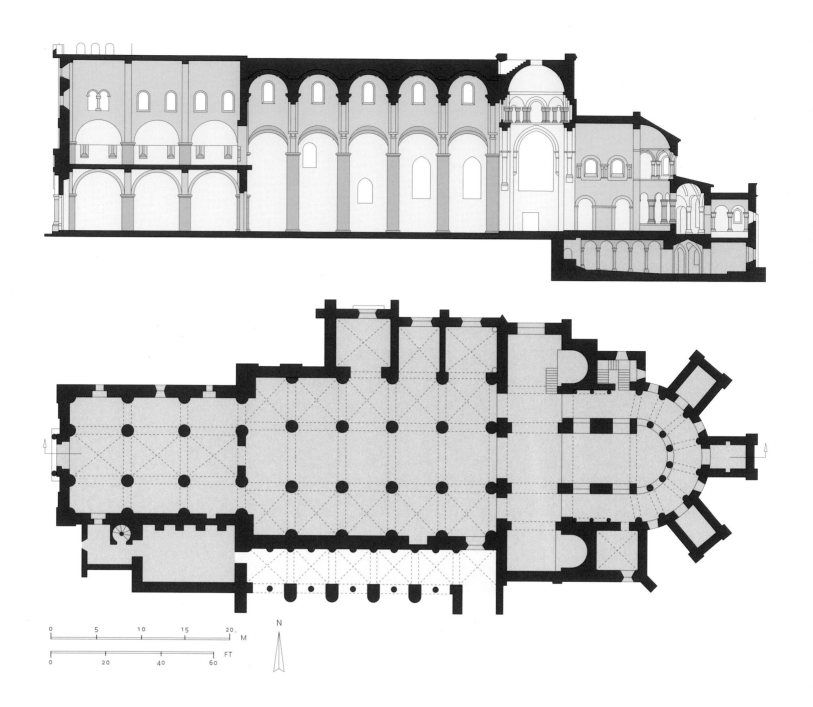

which open three rectangular chapels with flat back walls. It thus exemplifies the Romanesque chevet with ambulatory and radiating chapels.

Churches were adapted in this way to new liturgical needs. The pre-Romanesque church of Saint-Michel-de-Cuxa was enlarged by Abbot Oliba shortly before 1040. The chevet was rebuilt with an angular ambulatory skirting the main apse and leading to three apsidiole chapels. To the west two smaller churches were superposed. The lower, called Notre-Dame-de-la-Crèche, is dedicated to the Virgin, and is circular in plan, with a partially projecting apse and an annular vault supported on a central pillar and surrounding bays. The upper church is dedicated to the Trinity and is also central in plan. It is separated from the body of the main church by an atrium. A bell-tower rose on either side of the transept, though only the south tower survives. On the south side of the Trinity church and the atrium the characteristic pilaster-strip decoration has survived. The various sanctuaries display great liturgical unity, foreshadowing the liturgy of the Romanesque age.

The fully achieved Romanesque chevet
Saint-Philibert, Tournus, eleventh century, longitudinal section and plan. The two-storey narthex extends over three bays.

Page 37
A highly original vaulting system
Saint-Philibert, Tournus. The high masonry piers made vaulting of the nave difficult. The solution was a series of semicircular barrel vaults perpendicular to the axis of the nave.

A unified interior

Saint-Philibert, Tournus, ground floor of the narthex, eleventh century. The nave is groin-vaulted, and the aisles present transverse barrel vaults; these are carried by round piers 1.50 m in diameter. Semicircular piers built of small stones project from the walls. The ground floor communicates with the nave of the church via three arcades. Traces of painted mural decoration are visible.

Page 38 above
Audacious height

The circular piers of Saint-Philibert, Tournus, measuring 1.35 m in diameter and 9.35 m in height, carry the transverse ribs of the aisle groin vaults. The barrel vault of the nave is transversal and reaches a height of 18 m. It is carried on double-moulded diaphragm arches, offering clear testimony to the originality of the master mason.

Page 38 below left
A human figure

Saint-Philibert, Tournus, detail of carved decoration in the upper storey of the narthex, second quarter of the eleventh century. This block of stone is ornamented with a bearded head carved on the surface.

Page 38 below right
Evolution of the Corinthian capital

Saint-Philibert, Tournus, detail of a capital. Above the cord-moulding of the astragal, an array of palmettes covers the neck of the capital. The equilibrium of the Corinthian design is thus upset by the dense covering of the surfaces.

The First Northern Romanesque

In parallel with the first southern Romanesque, a very different style emerged in the north in the Ottonian period, with a distinct style of decoration and sense of architectural space. The essential feature of Ottonian architecture is the deployment of the paleo-Christian tradition on a very large scale. The monumentality of Ottonian church interiors is explained by the continued use of timber-framed roofs for the nave. As late as the mid-eleventh century only the aisles were vaulted. By contrast, the first southern Romanesque is low and narrow, as architects had yet to master the technique of vaulting large buildings in stone. The early experiments in vaulting required that the interior be divided up and the supports adapted to carry the weight.

Such internal division is notably absent from Ottonian buildings, which emphasise the continuity of the walls of the main chamber and the sturdy columns and

Incorporation of the transepts at Gernrode
Sankt Cyriakus, Gernrode, founded in 961, view of the east parts. The chevet comprises a single orthogonal bay continuing into a semicircular apse. It is raised over a crypt-hall of the same shape, which ends in a niche. The narrow transepts project relatively little and are merely a continuation of the nave and aisle, while the apse is substantially narrower. Each of the arms of the transepts has a small apsidiole chapel. The church of Sankt Cyriakus is typical of Ottonian architecture.

quadrangular piers that hold up the timber roof. Often a sense of rhythm is imparted by alternating piers and columns. In the Rhine area in particular, a double rhythm was frequently used, consisting of a single column between two quadrangular piers; in Saxony a triple rhythm was preferred, with two columns set between two quadrangular piers.

A rhythmic alternation of columns and piers can be seen in the former convent church of Sankt Cyriakus at Gernrode, founded in 961. Moreover, a new approach to interior space becomes evident here. The nave and aisles do not follow the Carolingian tradition of opening on to a full transept. Instead, the arms of the transept are separated from the crossing by arches. The galleries, although descended from Byzantine tradition, also fulfil a totally different function in this newly conceived spatial arrangement. In the lower sections of the nave's walls round arcades overlay piers and columns arranged according to the Rhineland tradition of alternating supports. Between the piers and the upper storey runs an arcaded gallery supported by slender, dainty columns. The rhythm thus imparted constitutes a radical break with the lofty bare walls traditional until that time.

This form of two-storey elevation, with arcades and clerestory, necessitated a number of projecting features, and thus facilitated the organisation of the Ottonian

A structure defined by bays
Sankt Cyriakus, Gernrode,
founded in 961, nave. The former
convent church presents nave and
aisles divided into bays by alternating monolithic columns and
rectangular piers. Transverse barrel vaults separate the transept
naves and the crossing/choir. A
flat timber roof stands over an elevation in which tribunes have now
established themselves.

A clearly defined structure
Sankt Michael, Hildesheim,
1010–1022/1033. The nave of the
former Benedictine monastery
church is divided into three bays,
each further divided by two
columns between two square
pillars. This alternating system
was much favoured in Saxony
during the Romanesque period.
There is a flat roof, and the two-
storey elevation comprises a
clerestory directly beneath it.
The expanse of plain, high walls
is one of the characteristics of
Ottonian architecture.

interior into bays; engaged columns could continue upwards from pier and dosseret
to receive on capitals the arcades framing the clerestory. The result was a very vig-
orous treatment of the interior as a whole. The structuring of the Romanesque interior space into bays was completed by the advent of projecting transverse arches and
stone-vaulted naves.

This transformation of architectural space is exemplified by the cathedral at
Speyer, an imposing building 133 m long and 50 m wide at the transept. The nave
was originally timber-roofed; rectangular piers with engaged columns support large
blind arcades. This architectural solution stands in contrast to the flat continuous
walls of the earlier period of Ottonian architecture, and introduced the division into
bays that was increasingly prevalent in the first southern Romanesque of the same
period. The vaulting of the nave (which was carried out in the second building stage,
Speyer II, at the end of the eleventh century) led to a division of the ground plan into
bays. Each bay in the nave had two corresponding side-aisle bays. This plan, based
on the underlying module of the crossing bay, brought the concept of an interior
space arranged into bays to its full fruition. Already in the first building phase
(Speyer I), the lateral aisles had been groin-vaulted and their walls had been graced
with small blind arcades. The transept extends the nave and is carefully articulated,

The art of stucco
Sankt Cyriakus, Gernrode, west wall of the Holy Sepulchre, circa 1100–1130. This building, a separate room in the south aisle, is decorated with stucco reliefs and figures relating to Easter. During the enactment of the mystery of the Resurrection it was used by nuns and clerics. Above the standing figure (probably Mary Magdalena) is the depiction of the Lamb of God; to the left stands John the Baptist as well as lions and a phoenix.

Rhythmic arcades and openings
Sankt Cyriakus, Gernrode, first half of the twelfth century, crossing, looking north-east. The nave is lit by a clerestory set high in the wall. Above the arcade are tribunes opening on to the nave through two groups of six little arcades, which match the two arcades of the lower storey. The differing rhythms articulate the division of space.

A clearly articulated westwork
Sankt Pantaleon, Cologne, late tenth century. The building comprises a square central tower with lateral extensions doing duty as a transept. A porch, which was heavily restored in the nineteenth century, projects westwards; it is flanked by two slender turrets set on a rectangular base, which are first octagonal then round in section. Pilaster strips and blind arcades betray classical and Italian influence.

divided into three equal parts: the two arms of the transept, with chapels in the thickness of their east walls, and the crossing, for which an octagonal lantern tower had originally been planned. The choir consists of a single orthogonal bay originally framed by two staircase towers, and prefigures the 'harmonic chevet' characteristic of the major buildings of the Romanesque period. The chevet was reconstructed about thirty-five years after the consecration in 1060; the walls of the crypt were reinforced and the choir was extended to create a semicircular apse, decorated inside and out with blind arcades and an arcaded gallery high up on the wall. The latter is found in the first southern Romanesque as a decorative motif; it was frequently used in the twelfth century in the Rhineland and northern Italy. In this second campaign, two bell-towers were built to replace the staircase towers that had flanked the old choir. They are similar to the campaniles of the first southern style, from which they have inherited their decorative Lombard bands. Each band underlines one of the registers of windows in the upper parts of the tower.

A crypt-hall, groin-vaulted between transverse arches, lies under the whole area of the chevet and transept. The west part comprises a porch surmounted by a gallery. There was presumably a second tower matching the one at the east crossing. This prefigures the architectural compositions that subsequently developed in the central Rhineland, notably at Maria Laach, Mainz and Worms. The projecting archivolts of the main portal are another feature widely employed in later Romanesque churches.

The decoration is inspired by classical art, transmitted either directly or through the Carolingian heritage. Unlike the homogeneous ornamentation of the first southern Romanesque, eleventh-century northern decoration is extremely varied, and is not confined to the outside of buildings. Despite increasingly prevalent southern influences during the period 1025–1035, this aspect of the Ottonian tradition proved very durable. Its effect is clearly to be seen in the buildings of the central and upper Rhineland such as Limburg an der Haardt, Speyer, Ottmarsheim, and Sankt Maria und Markus at Mittelzell on the island of Reichenau on Lake Constance. The innovations introduced in these buildings prepared the transition from Ottonian to Romanesque architecture.

External volumes were also modified. Ottonian architecture inherited a Carolingian feature: the development of east and west ends. Modification of the east end was necessitated by the cult of relics. Large-scale extension of the west end also took place. This involved a large structure called a westwork, or a retrochoir with apse, similar in appearance to the east choir.

A highly developed form of this bipolarity is to be found in Sankt Michael at Hildesheim. The church was founded in 1010 by Bernward, tutor to Otto III and Bishop of Hildesheim from 993 to 1022. It presents two analogous terminations, each of which has a transept with a lantern tower at the crossing. The crossing in each case is symmetrical, making it one of the earliest examples of its kind. Symmetrical transepts and lantern towers played a major role in later Romanesque architecture. In general, the lantern tower at the crossing stood above a dome on squinches of the kind found in Speyer cathedral and the abbey church of Limburg an der Haardt (completed in 1045); it slowly evolved towards the octagonal, like the transept towers of the first southern Romanesque. But the imposing towers of the southern style are here replaced by towers alongside the choir and by slender staircase turrets.

Page 45 above
Simplicity of form
Sankt Georg, Reichenau-Oberzell, 888–913, chevet. The transept is integrated with the side-aisles, and the nave opens on to a flat-ended chevet; it is so high because it is over a crypt. The squat, square tower is set over the crossing. This design is characteristic of the pre-Romanesque churches of Reichenau.

Superlative murals

Sankt Georg, Reichenau-Oberzell, 888–913. The nave presents a row of columns and abundant painted decoration (second half of the tenth century), of which only that of the lateral walls has survived. The narrative scenes show scenes from the life of Christ, and are framed by wide *trompe-l'œil* friezes of meanders. Despite modern restoration, this remains one of the most important sets of frescoes of the pre-Romanesque.

Polychrome plaster at Hildesheim
Sankt Michael, Hildesheim, choir
screen on the north side of the
choir, around 1200. Between two
ornamented friezes stand a series
of arcades resting on slender
colonnettes. The shafts are decorated with chevron mouldings or
geometrical motifs. The capitals,
too, are sculpted, and feature
projecting abacuses on which rest
little winged angels. The colouring
is a modern reconstruction of
the original state.

Romanesque Architecture

The term Romanesque emerged in the early nineteenth century in Normandy, in a period of high enthusiasm for monumental archaeology and the rediscovery of medieval art. By the eleventh century, the architectural forms of Romanesque in western Europe were highly developed. The entire building was vaulted, and the thrust of the vaults contained by buttresses. Particular attention was lavished on the design of the chevet with its numerous apses. The façade was often framed by towers. Moreover, sculpted decoration numbers among the main characteristics of Romanesque religious architecture. Toulouse and the Spanish kingdoms were centres from which this new art radiated. In the past, researchers have sought to establish which of the two came first. Today we know that interaction and exchange played a vital role in the spread of Romanesque art.

Romanesque architecture in France can be divided into two stylistic groups. The first of these was current in the late eleventh century and the early decades of the twelfth. It was the product of technical and functional requirements. These build-ings have a nave and two or four side-aisles, projecting transepts with apsidioles, a chevet comprising ambulatory and radiating chapels, and a façade framed by towers. Above the groin-vaulted aisles rise tribunes with pointed tunnel vaults. The aisles and tribunes receive direct light; the barrel-vaulted nave receives only in-direct light. This architectural series comprises collegiate churches, abbeys and cathedrals. The most striking examples are on the pilgrimage route of Santiago de Compostela: Saint-Sernin in Toulouse, Sainte-Foy at Conques, Saint-Martial at Limoges and Saint-Martin at Tours.

The second group is composed of churches in southern and western France that are not barrel- or groin-vaulted but roofed with rows of domes. This group has often been thought to show the direct influence of Islamic or Byzantine art. These buildings have no side-aisles; the nave is very wide. There are sometimes pro-jecting transepts (as at Solignac, Souillac and Angoulême cathedral). The apse is as wide as the nave, and there are apsidal chapels in some cases. The nave is covered with a row of domes on pendentives, resting on very wide, slightly pointed arches carried on massive piers. The most remarkable examples of this style in western France are the cathedrals of Périgueux, Cahors and Angoulême, and a series of monuments in the Limousin, the Saintonge, Périgord, and at Moissac (Quercy) and in Guyenne, all of them built in or around the first and second decades of the twelfth century.

Angoulême cathedral (begun in 1110) perfectly exemplifies this group. Here we find the oldest kind of dome, which is also to be seen in the west bay of the cathedral of Saint-Michel at Périgueux and in the naves of Cahors cathedral and the former abbey church of Souillac. The research of Pierre Dubourg-Noves has shown that, in the first bay at Angoulême, the four arches carrying the dome rested on four sturdy piers and that the base of the side walls presented a corbel table and pilaster strips. Unfortunately, nineteenth-century rebuilding gave this dome the same appearance as that of the others. The latter were constructed not with rubble infill but in regular courses, and raised on double arches supported by piers with engaged columns. The side walls present a blind arcade decorated with sculpted capitals. There is a further dome at the very wide crossing; the transepts originally ended in bell-towers of unequal size. The smaller, south bell-tower no longer exists; the north tower, though drastically restored in the nineteenth century, displays remarkable capitals at ground-floor level. The very deep chevet has four lateral chapels arranged two on either side of a large axial window.

Another major building, the cathedral of Saint-Front (after 1120) in Périgueux, has much to tell us about the construction of such domes. Here two buildings on dif-

Left

Bishop Bernward's door
Cathedral, Hildesheim, bronze doors, circa 1015, 4.72 m x 1.12 m (each leaf). The doors, which were probably originally made for the church of Sankt Michael, are divided into eight horizontal registers, each of which contains a scene from the Old or New Testament. The fact that each leaf was cast as a single piece testifies to the mastery of the craftsman involved.

Right

The genealogy of Christ
Sankt Michael, Hildesheim, detail of painted wooden ceiling, mid-thirteenth century. The paintings show the Tree of Jesse, beginning with Adam and Eve.

Masterful buttressing
Notre-Dame-du-Port, Clermont-Ferrand, begun circa 1100, interior of the dome from the crossing. Four piers flanked by semicircular columns take the weight of the great arches of the crossing; above the arches are high walls with triple bays. These in their turn support the octagonal dome on squinches. Each transept comprises one narrow orthogonal bay with a quadrant vault that buttresses the dome. From the outside, this constitutes a single massive rectangle out of which rises the bell-tower.

ferent axes abut: a basilica with bell-tower, and a domed church of Greek-cross plan. The major reconstruction work effected in the nineteenth century was largely confined to the elevation and to the treatment of masonry. Originally, rubble domes of various sizes were built, with four or five regular courses at the base for strengthening. The domes in place today are similar but constructed in courses throughout. The pendentives are all carried on springing stones; they originally had eleven springing courses at their bases with the remainder perpendicular to the curve of the pendentives. The gallery beneath the windows has been preserved, and the lower part of the piers carrying the domes has been hollowed out to create four smaller piers surrounding a cruciform internal space.

The roofing at Saint-Front is quite different from that of the cathedral at Le Puy where the domes are carried not on pendentives but on squinches. By the eleventh century the cathedral had become the centre of an important Marian pilgrimage. It comprised a nave and aisles divided into four bays and barrel-vaulted. The very spacious transepts were also barrel-vaulted. Within the end wall of each transept was an apsidiole, surmounted by deep tribunes. At the crossing, a bell-tower rises above the dome on half-dome squinches. The termination of the extended choir is semicircular within and rectangular without; it is framed by two very narrow chapels. This layout preserves most of the features of pre-Romanesque architecture. In the twelfth century the barrel vault of the nave was replaced by domical vaults. They are in eight webs, on hemispherical squinches resting on quarter-circle cornices whose central section is cantilevered. To north and south, wide bays pierced between the squinches light the nave. This design should be compared, as Marcel Durliat has shown not with Islamic architecture, but with the domes of Saint-Martin-d'Ainay in Lyons; it was developed in the Auvergne, around Lyons and in Provence between 1075 and 1200.

Page 49 above left
An airy interior
Cathedral of Saint-Pierre, Angoulême, from 1110, section. In the first bay, four great arches carry the dome resting on massive pillars. This is the oldest form of dome on pendentives, and is probably of Oriental inspiration. The cathedral was thoroughly restored in the nineteenth century.

Page 49 above right
The row of domes as nave roof
Saint-Pierre, Angoulême, plan. The nave is roofed with three domes each around 10 m in diameter. The transept projects strongly, and the choir is some 26 m deep and 12 m wide; it opens on to the four radiating chapels and a large axial window.

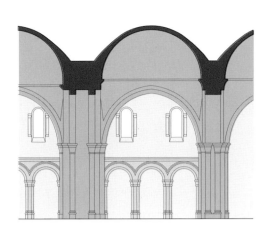

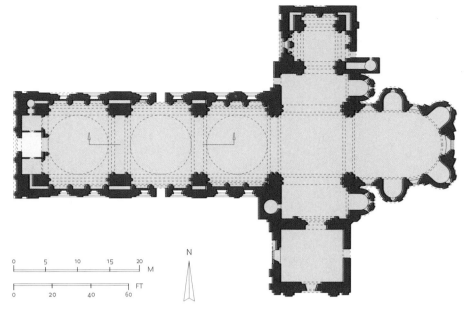

| 0 | 5 | 10 | 15 | 20 |
| --- | --- | --- | --- | --- | M |

| 0 | 20 | 40 | 60 |
| --- | --- | --- | --- | FT |

N

A formula for western France
Saint-Pierre, Angoulême. The last two bays of the nave have taller domes without rubble infill; the stones are laid in courses. The two-level arches are set on engaged columns crowned by sculpted capitals. In the region between the Garonne and the Loire, the nave without aisles roofed with a series of domes was to become widely adopted.

THE DIFFUSION OF ROMANESQUE

Architecture in the West: Churches and Pilgrimages

Page 51
Head reliquary of the holy pope Alexander
Stavelot, circa 1145, silver-gilt, *cloisonné* enamels, pearls and cabochons. On a shrine shaped like a portable altar with enamels showing various saints stands the bust of Alexander. Habit and haircut are reminiscent of Roman Imperial portraits – an example of the interest the Middle Ages took in classical culture. (Musées Royaux d'Art et d'Histoire, Brussels)

The Last Judgement
Sainte-Foy, Conques, detail of the tympanum of the west door, 1120–1135. The last trump has sounded, and the souls of the damned are cast into Hell. Here horror and despair reign: lust, mendacity, adultery, avarice and pride are punished with tortures whose terror is perfectly expressed in these bodies distorted with pain.

The Pilgrimage Routes

The Middle Ages were a time of pilgrimage. Particularly during the eleventh and twelfth centuries, the phenomenon attained an intensity unique in Christian civilisation. Pilgrimage is a journey to a sacred place, a place of devotion, where the pilgrim hopes to obtain divine grace. The pilgrim alone determines the date and destination of the journey. In the Middle Ages the route normally comprised several stages, each ending in a holy place and constituting a partial pilgrimage in itself. Each pilgrimage was an act of faith; the road was perilous and the pilgrim's life could be at stake. As the number of pilgrims grew, more sacred places joined the list of destinations. But three goals were of prime importance: the Holy Sepulchre in the Holy Land, the tomb of Saint Peter in Rome, and the tomb of Saint James (Sant'Iago) at Santiago de Compostela in northwestern Spain.

Saint James 'the Great' was one of the Apostles, and plays an important role in the Gospels and the Acts of the Apostles. He was beheaded around A.D. 41–44 and the site of his tomb was forgotten. However, according to the tradition recorded in the *Concordia de Antealtares* (1077), the site of the tomb was miraculously revealed in the early ninth century to a Spanish hermit named Pelagius, who had taken up residence near the church of San Felix. When Alfonso II (791–842), King of Asturias, learnt of the discovery, he immediately had three churches built on the site.

In a period of incessant war and strife, notably between Christendom and Islam, Alfonso II brought to his kingdom an artistic and cultural renaissance; it was based on renewed prosperity, and entailed cultural and commercial exchanges with the court of Charlemagne. The discovery of the relics made Saint James a symbol of the protection of Christian Spain. He was represented as a powerful mounted warrior combating the Muslims, and was given the nickname *Matamoros* (the killer of Moors). Donations and pilgrims flooded in, and a town was built for and around the mausoleum.

The pilgrim routes were described in the numerous guides which advised and assisted the pilgrim step by step. The *Pilgrim's Guide to Santiago de Compostela*, an extract from Book V of the *Codex Calixtinus* (1139), is among the most interesting of these, and particularly useful in acquainting us with the different routes to Compostela. There were four such routes: the *via Tolosona*, the *via Podensis*, the *via Lemovicensis* and the *via Turonensis*.

The *via Tolosana* was generally followed by pilgrims coming from Italy or from the Orient, and those following the Mediterranean coast. It led from Arles via Toulouse to Puente la Reina. The first staging post was the cathedral at Arles, where pilgrims prayed and meditated at the tomb of Saint Trophimus. Continuing westward, they reached Saint-Gilles-du-Gard and venerated Saint Giles, the patron saint of that town. Before reaching Toulouse, they passed through numerous other holy places where relics were conserved, such as Saint-Guilhem-le-Désert, where the body of Saint Guilhem lay, Murat-sur-Vèbre and Castres. At Toulouse the pilgrim would venerate the body of Saint Serninus, bishop and martyr; thereafter the guide

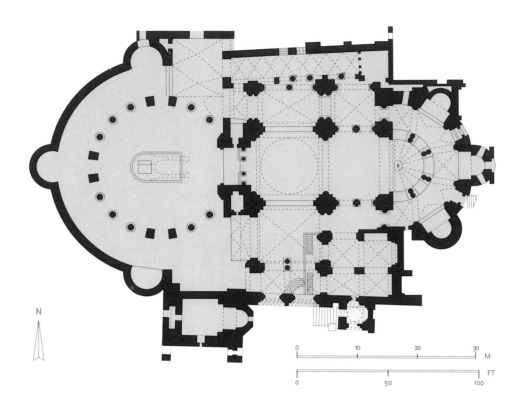

N

A major Crusader building
The Church of the Holy Sepulchre, Jerusalem, rebuilt in the twelfth century, plan. A monumental rotunda with tribunes incorporating three semicircular chapels dominates the plan. This unit adjoins a church presenting a crossing and a choir leading to an ambulatory with three radiating chapels. At the crossing is a lantern resting on pendentives and crowned with a dome. The great originality of this construction is the grafting of the rotunda on to a basilican church.

Page 55

An imposing Languedoc tower
Cathedral of Saint-Trophîme, Arles, rebuilt from circa 1150. The square bell-tower presents three storeys, each set in from the one below and clearly defined by cornices. The first two levels are decorated with Lombard bands and the third with fluted pilasters bearing sculpted capitals. An attic storey completes the tower.

recommends visiting 'the bodies of the blessed martyrs Tiberius, Modestus and Florentius ... they rest on the banks of the [River] Hérault in a very handsome sepulchre' before continuing through Pibrac, Auch, Morlaas, Lescar, Pau, La Commande and Oloron-Sainte-Marie. They would then cross the valley of the Aspe and the Somport pass. Pilgrims coming from the east and passing through Montpellier sometimes preferred to cross Catalonia rather than the Languedoc. From there, both routes reached Puente la Reina.

The second route, the *via Podensis*, was that from Le Puy to Ostabat on the Spanish side of the Pyrenees, where the four routes joined. This was mainly followed by pilgrims coming from Lyons, Vienne, Valence or from Clermont-Ferrand, Issoire, Sauxillanges and Brioude. From its starting point in Le Puy, the route led over the Aubrac massif, through Perse, Bessuejouls and the gorges of the Dourdou. There was a halt at Conques, where the relics of Saint Faith are conserved in the basilica. The road continued through Figeac, where the pilgrim could turn aside and visit Rocamadour, Marcilhac, Cahors and Le Montat before rejoining the route through Moissac, Lectoure, Condom, Eauze, Aire-sur-l'Adour, Orthez and Sauveterre-de-Béarn, and finally reaching Ostabat.

The *via Lemovicensis* started in Vézelay and passed through Saint-Léonard-de-Noblat. Pilgrims began by venerating the relics of Mary Magdalene at Vézelay. Then they went via La Charité-sur-Loire, Nevers, Noirlac, Neuvy-Saint-Sépulcre and Gargilesse or via Bourges, Charost, Déols, Châteauroux and Argenton-sur-Creuse to Saint-Léonard, where they prayed over the relics of the hermit saint. Thence the *jacquets* (pilgrims of Saint James, or Jacques in French) travelled to Limoges. From there they went to La Réole and Mont-de-Marsan, passing through Saint-Jean-de-Côle and stopping at Périgueux to visit the relics of Saint Frontus in the cathedral. There, the pilgrim could make a detour through Trémolat along the Dordogne before arriving in Ostabat.

The fourth route was the *via Turonensis*. From Paris, it passed through Orléans, where the 'wooden cross and chalice of Saint Euvertus, bishop and confessor' were preserved in the church of Sainte-Croix. Pilgrims could also journey through

Inspired by Roman triumphal arches

Saint-Gilles-du-Gard, late twelfth century, west façade. The west façade presents three portals, the largest being the axial doorway. The columns set off from the walls lead up to an entablature crowned by a historiated frieze. Between them, the statues in niches framed by fluted pilasters carry a second entablature. The composition offers remarkable perspective effects of a kind associated with Roman architecture.

Chartres to Tours (Tours was the setting of several of the miracles of Saint Martin). They would then go to Ingrandes and thence to Poitiers, to pray before the relics of Saint Hilary, before choosing between two routes, one of which led through Angoulême, the other through Saintes. If they chose the latter, they would halt at Saint-Jean-d'Angély for prayer and meditation before the 'the venerable head of Saint John the Baptist which was brought by holy men from Jerusalem to the place called Angély in the Poitevin'. The *jacquets* made a further halt at Saintes for the body of Saint Eutropus, bishop and martyr, before heading for Blaye 'on the shore of the sea, ... [where] the protection of Saint Romanus must be invoked' and stopped at Bordeaux for the relics of Saint Severinus. They had only to traverse Saint-Paul-lès-Dax before reaching Ostabat.

From this point, pilgrims took the *camino francés* (French route) across the Basque country to reach the cross of Charles, the first prayer-halt on the road to Compostela. The major Spanish itineraries were relatively easy, though the *jacquet* in Spain could not miss 'the body of the blessed Dominic, confessor, who constructed the road between Nareja and Redecilla where he reposes. One should also visit the bodies of the Saints Facundus and Primitivus, whose basilica was built by Charlemagne ...; thence, one must go to León to pay one's respects to the blessed Isidore, bishop, confessor and doctor, who instituted a very devout rule for the ecclesiastical cleric, persuaded the Spanish people as a whole of his doctrine and honoured the Holy Church in every way by his fruitful works.' Pilgrims continued through Pamplona to Puente la Reina, then, passing through Estella, took the road for Rioja. The route through Castile and León was similarly punctuated by relics and holy places.

At last the *jacquet* entered Galicia, and Santiago de Compostela beckoned. There were sixteen 'stages' on the Spanish route to Compostela, each with its own rituals. At Compostela itself, several rituals had to be accomplished. At the Cisa Pass, the pilgrim placed a cross on the ground, after 'bending the knee and gazing towards the homeland of Saint James and making orison'. Then the pilgrims plunged into the cold Atlantic water to purify themselves 'for love of the Apostle'. Finally, they had to transport a block of chalk from Mont Cerebro to Castañola; these stones were then brought by carts to Compostela. Pilgrims brought offerings that enriched the treasure of the sanctuary. They put on new garments before undergoing the purification of the soul, after which they received a document testifying to their visit to Santiago de Compostela and the expiation of their sins.

Page 57 centre left
Cathedral of the Black Virgin
Notre-Dame, Le Puy-en-Velay, largely twelfth century. The square detached bell-tower stands on the side of the chevet; its 56 m height dominates the building. The storeys each set in from the one below and the high windows produce a resemblance to the bell-towers of the Limousin. To the right of it is the crossing dome, refashioned as a lantern tower by the architect Mallay in the nineteenth century.

Page 57 centre right
A legendary site
Saint-Michel, Aiguilhe, near Le Puy-en-Velay. Set on an 85 m basalt needle (*aiguille*) after which the village is named, the oratory is reached by a staircase of 250 steps. The original building dated from the second half of the tenth century. In the late eleventh or early twelfth century a sort of narthex and a circular gallery were built, their plan necessarily following the shape of the site; the gallery serves as a nave.

Romanesque carved decoration
San Martín, Frómista, eleventh century. The church presents a nave and aisles extending into a tripartite apse. The striking features of the building are the small-scale masonry of the walls, the presence at the crossing of a dome on squinches surmounted by an octagonal tower, and the two cylindrical turrets that frame the façade. These elements characterise the first southern Romanesque; the rich ornamentation of capitals and modillions announces the advent of Romanesque monumental sculpture.

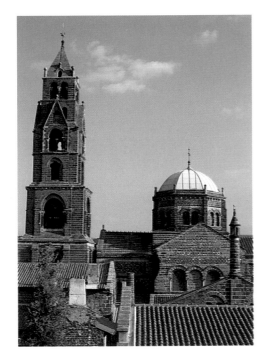

The centre of one style of Burgundian Romanesque
Vézelay, overall view. In the tenth and eleventh centuries, Burgundy occupied a central place in the religious life of the West. Two types of architecture were born there. The first derives from the Cluniac order, whose influence grew rapidly from the late eleventh century on; the second developed at Anzy-le-Duc and at Vézelay.

A polychrome façade
Notre-Dame, Le Puy-en-Velay, façade reconstructed on Romanesque lines in the nineteenth century. The façade stands above a monumental staircase; above its three portals are three carefully articulated storeys. The solidity of the walls is relieved by blind arcades and false niches. The alternation in voussoirs and masonry of red and black stone, and the marquetry of red, white and black stones in the gables, constitute one of the most original features of Romanesque architecture in the Auvergne and Velay.

Page 59
Polychrome mural decoration
Notre-Dame, Le Puy-en-Velay, detail of the galleries of the cloister adjoining the cathedral. They feature sculpted decoration complemented by polychrome masonry of highly ornamental effect. Some historiated capitals present figures or the symbols of the Evangelists, but foliated capitals predominate. Their combination of geometrical motifs, volutes, interwoven foliated scrolls and acanthus leaves is typical of the Auvergne and Velay during the second half of the twelfth century.

The Architecture

From the late eleventh century and throughout the twelfth, a great tide of building engulfed the Santiago route. Monasteries, abbey churches, basilicas and collegiate churches rose up along the route, revealing a newly mature Romanesque style resplendent in its sculptural decoration, which proliferated in cloisters and façades.

The intense religiosity of the period gave rise to large-scale and sometimes highly ambitious constructions. In the second half of the twelfth century Le Puy cathedral was extended in order to accommodate the steady development in the Marian cult of which it was the centre. Two supplementary bays were then added to the west end of the nave; they stood on top of an imposing porch preceded by a monumental stairway, which together compensated for the steeply sloping position. This architectural solution is also found in the church of San Michele della Chiusa in Piedmont, which is built on a very confined site on the rocky summit of Mont Pirchiriano. The sanctuary here was extended to the east by the addition of a

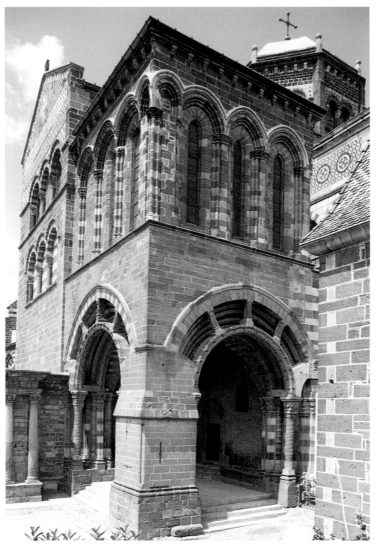

A dome carried on squinches
Notre-Dame, Le Puy-en-Velay, circa 1150, internal view of the domes of the nave. These are eight-webbed domes set on hemispherical squinches. The squinches in their turn rest on a corbel table whose central part is cantilevered. To north and south, large windows sited between the squinches light the nave. This architectural formula was developed between 1110 and 1115 at Saint-Martin d'Ainay (Lyons), then at Saint-Philibert, Tournus.

Sturdy proportions
Notre-Dame, Le Puy-en-Velay, the Porche du For on the south-east side of the cathedral, late twelfth – early thirteenth century. The porch stands at the junction of the aisle and the south transept. It is entered through arcades, each of which is duplicated by a large free-standing concentric arch, linked to the higher arch by three small pilasters. A massive masonry pier supports the voussoirs in the south-west corner; on the other sides, they rest on fluted piers or diapered columns on rectangular bases.

Sainte-Foy, Conques, late eleventh century. Located in an inaccessible spot, the abbey became renowned through its relics of the saint, stolen by the monks in about 880 from the neighbouring abbey. In the Middle Ages such deeds were not uncommon, and meant that the guardians of relics had to keep a close watch on their treasures. The building exemplifies the so-called 'pilgrimage' architecture.

chevet, which similarly rose from a monumental staircase. A further though much later parallel might also be cited, one dating from the transition to the Gothic style: Mont-Saint-Michel.

Amid this architectural efflorescence, a new type of building appeared on the Santiago pilgrimage route. It seems to have exercised considerable influence over churches such as Saint-Martin at Tours, Saint-Martial at Limoges, Sainte-Foy at Conques, Saint-Sernin at Toulouse and the cathedral of Santiago de Compostela itself. In the late eleventh century and early twelfth centuries, abbey and collegiate churches and cathedrals frequently adopted a similar plan, with two or four side-aisles and a chevet with ambulatory and radiating chapels. The tall towers framing the façade provided an imposing west end. The chevet provided a subtle harmony of volumes centring on the height of the ambulatory and the radiating apsidioles, whose orientation contrasted with that of the transepts. The main nave, much higher than the aisles, was vaulted with a semicircular barrel vault with transverse arches, while the aisles were groin-vaulted. The aisles carried wide tribunes opening through arcades on to the nave. Light flooded in through tribune and aisle windows.

The origins of this 'pilgrimage basilica' style are obscure. Sainte-Foy at Conques is recognised as the first of the series, though it was built before the end of the eleventh century, and the new convention established itself around 1120. The countryside around Conques is infertile and its climate unwelcoming, so the arrival of the body of Saint Faith was the salvation of the area, bringing with it not merely divine favour but the assurance of material revenue. Sainte-Foy has all the

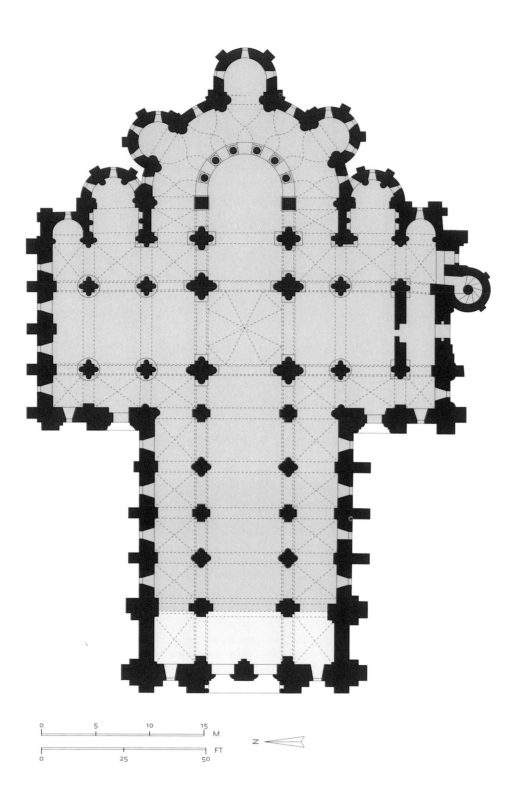

A compact pilgrimage church
Sainte-Foy, Conques, late
eleventh century, plan of the
abbey church. There is a barrel
vault in the nave and groin vaults
in the aisles. The transept is
divided into nave and aisles and
opens on to a chevet with ambulatory and radiating chapels; each
arm of the transept has two
apsidioles, of which the outer is
the smaller. The plan perfectly
fulfils the requirements of a
pilgrimage church.

characteristics of the pilgrimage churches, notably the high tribunes above the
side-aisles of nave, transept and choir. But it is on a relatively small scale: the very
short nave with single side-aisles has only six bays, and the transept has not yet
attained the scale and development to be seen in the cathedral of Santiago de
Compostela or the church of Saint-Sernin in Toulouse. It has only east and west
aisles, the east one being smaller; they do not continue around the end of the
transept arms. The nave has a semicircular barrel vault on wide transverse arches,
buttressed by the quadrant vaults of the tribunes. The latter have large windows
with semicircular arches. The aisles are groin-vaulted.

The crossing dome is carried on eight ribs, and was, like the bell-tower, constructed in the fourteenth century. The most original feature of the church is the

The Romanesque echelon apse
Sainte-Foy, Conques, late eleventh century, chevet. Above the chapels and ambulatory rises the apse, which is ornamented with tall column buttresses joined by a blind arcade beneath the cornice. The octagonal tower at the crossing, which features a staircase turret, dominates the chevet as a whole.

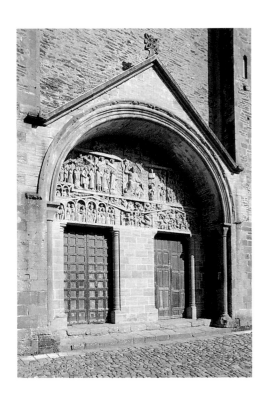

A didactic tympanum
Sainte-Foy, Conques, tympanum of west portal, circa 1120–1135. In the early twelfth century sculptural decoration spread throughout the Romanesque church. Tympanums became the site of large-scale iconographic programmes. At Conques, the Last Judgment admonishes the passer-by to enter the House of God.

chevet. Two apsidioles are built into each transept; one of these is relatively large, the other a mere niche in the wall of the arm. This arrangement is similar to that of the 'Benedictine chevet', with its axial apse flanked by echelon apsidal chapels. However, the choir ambulatory gives on to three radiating chapels, one of which, the axial chapel, is longer than the other two. It thus combines the Benedictine plan of echelon chapels grafted on to the transept with an ambulatory and radiating chapels. A complement of five chapels was customary in the pilgrim churches, and the combination is explained by a change in plan during construction, or the existence of two successive states. The latter case would be analogous to that of La Charité-sur-Loire, where the original Benedictine plan was enriched by a vast ambulatory with radiating chapels. But this second hypothesis seems unlikely,

Spacious tribunes
Sainte-Foy, Conques, late eleventh – early twelfth century, north aisle and transept looking west. Above the arcade of the nave is a tribune gallery. Its large double bays bring light into the nave. Tribune galleries form part of the formula of the pilgrimage church; at Conques they are reached by a very tight spiral staircase.

given the homogeneity of materials: big, regular courses of red sandstone from the Nauviale quarries are found throughout the chevet.

The churches of Saint-Sernin in Toulouse and Santiago de Compostela are exactly contemporaneous. They are the first true examples of pilgrim churches. By the date of its consecration in 1096, Saint-Sernin must have been almost finished, and since work on the cathedral at Santiago had begun in 1075, it too must have been well advanced by the later date.

The cathedral of Santiago de Compostela was constructed on the site of the former church of Antealtares, built by Alfonso II. The regular, symmetrical plan of the basilica is identical to that of Conques, as were those of almost all the pilgrim churches. The Latin-cross nave is preceded by a narthex and flanked by aisles, and leads to a transept with four chapels oriented to the east. The transept in its turn opens on to an ambulatory with five radiating chapels. Transverse arches carry the

Flooded with light: the crossing
Sainte-Foy, Conques, internal
view of the crossing. The eight-
ribbed dome at the crossing, set
on squinches, is a fourteenth-
century addition, as is the bell-
tower above it. The spandrels on
the choir side are decorated with
angels, and those on the nave
side with heads of Saints Peter and
Paul. The transepts are each lit by
two large windows surmounted
by an oculus.

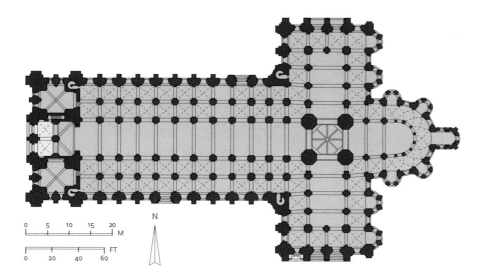

The Romanesque echelon apse
Saint-Sernin, Toulouse, 1060–1150,
chevet. Five tall chapels open off
the ambulatory between wide
windows, each surmounted by an
oculus. The walls are brick, with
ashlar used for the window
frames, cornices and buttresses.
The tall, thin colonnettes, laid
with the grain of the stone
vertical, frame the chapels and
emphasise the vertical dimension,
while the series of bays and
modillions underlines the horizontal dimension of the chevet.

The perfected cruciform plan
The church of Saint-Sernin at
Toulouse is in Latin cross plan.
The nave and four aisles open on
to a projecting transept, around
which the aisles continue. At the
chevet the ambulatory leads to
five radiating chapels, and there
are two apsidioles on each arm of
the transept. Here, the formula of
the pilgrimage church attains
maturity.

Page 67 above left
Two-storey nave elevation
The tribune galleries of Saint-
Sernin occupy the full width of
the side-aisles; large double bays
bring light to the nave. The role of
the tribunes is not clear, but given
their narrow access stairs and
the structure of their floors, they
cannot have accommodated many
pilgrims.

Page 67 right
Vertical emphases
Saint-Sernin, Toulouse, external
view. The gradation of the roof-
levels, the buttresses punctuating
the openings, and the decorative
framing of the bays and portals
create a remarkable articulation of
volumes. The great lantern tower
rests on the massive piers of
the crossing; it was restored by
Viollet-le-Duc in the nineteenth
century, to highly controversial
effect.

barrel vault of the nave, which is buttressed by the quadrant vaults of the tribune. The very wide transept is flanked by aisles on three sides. The chevet consists of a wide axial chapel, whose plan is semicircular within and square without. The great novelty at Santiago is the presence of tall, deep tribunes with large windows. They open on to the nave through large bays, which are divided by coupled columns and framed by a discharging arch. In this way, the nave receives indirect light from both tribunes and aisles. The original Romanesque lantern-tower has been replaced by a *cimborio* at the crossing. The whole is completed by two façade towers, with two further towers at the angle of nave and transept.

Work began with the chevet, more precisely with the axial chapel, which was consecrated as the chapel of the Saviour around 1075. An interruption was caused in 1088 by a quarrel between the Bishop, Diego Peláez, and the chapter; work began again in about 1100 under Bishop Diego Gelmírez. Five years later the chevet, the ambulatory, and the arms of the transept (with their four apsidioles, two on either side) were consecrated at the same time as the eight altars of the chevet. The cloister, which is no longer extant, was begun in 1124 by Diego Gelmírez, who was

Admonitory decoration
Saint-Sernin, Toulouse, detail of
a capital, late eleventh century.
Between the plain astragal and
the abacus with its palmette
ornament, the neck is carved with
two upright billy-goats on either
side of a plant motif.

by then Archbishop; it was reconstructed in Gothic style in the sixteenth century. The basilica was completed in 1122 or 1124, and was consecrated in 1211 by Archbishop Pedro Muñiz.

The church of Saint-Sernin in Toulouse closely follows the Santiago plan, differing only in having double side-aisles in the nave, and façade towers in line with the side-aisles. This was also true of Saint-Martin in Tours, which was, alas, almost wholly demolished in 1798. Its only vestiges are one of the façade towers, known as the Tour du Trésor or Tour de l'Horloge (Treasury or Clock Tower), and the north transept tower, known as the Tour de Charlemagne (Charlemagne's Tower). Excavation has revealed the foundations of an ambulatory with radiating chapels. The archaeologist Charles Lelong has defined a nave more than 21 m high, similar in that

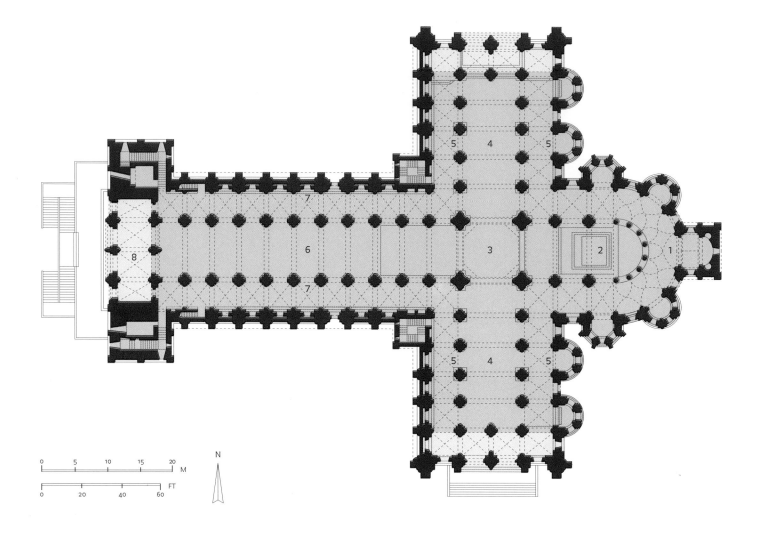

respect to Saint-Sernin (21.1 m) and Santiago de Compostela (22 m). The large arcades were 10.8 m high, whereas those of Saint-Sernin and Santiago were 9.5 m only. The church of Saint-Martial at Limoges has suffered the same fate as Saint-Martin. We know it only from plans made prior to its demolition, and by a section drawing of the transept and a longitudinal section of the building as a whole. It differed from the other pilgrimage churches in having a bell-tower in the centre of its west façade.

These were large buildings designed to accommodate immense crowds; the cathedral at Santiago de Compostela measures 97 m in length. The popularity of the cult of relics meant that large numbers of altars were set up in the chevet, and systems of circulation were required. The faithful entered by the side-aisle on one side, continued around the transept aisles into the ambulatory, and left via the aisle on the other side. This meant that the liturgical activities of the monastic community could continue serenely despite the huge crowds of pilgrims flowing through the church.

The greatest pilgrimage church
Santiago de Compostela, plan of the cathedral, 1075–1122 or 1124. The cathedral of Saint James (Sant'lago) is in Latin cross plan, with a broad nave and single aisles. The aisles continue around the transept, which is on the same scale as the nave. There are five radiating chapels opening on to the ambulatory. This arrangement meant that pilgrims could circulate while liturgical activity was going on.
1 Ambulatory
2 Choir
3 Crossing
4 Transept
5 Transept aisle
6 Nave
7 Aisle
8 Pórtico de la Gloria

The Pórtico de la Gloria
Santiago de Compostela, cathedral, Pórtico de la Gloria, central portal leading to the nave, carved by Master Mateo, 1188–1200. The tympanum shows a combination of the Last Judgment and the Apocalypse. Christ is flanked by the Evangelists, carrying their symbols, and the Redeemed. In the archivolt are the twenty-four Elders of the Apocalypse. Above the lintel, angels show the symbols of the Passion. In front of the trumeau sits Saint James, the church's patron.

Conventional buttressing
Santiago de Compostela, cathedral, 1075–1122/1124, interior. The barrel vault on transverse ribs springs from columns engaged in the piers. It is buttressed by the quadrant vaults of the aisles.

Façades: The Triumphal Arch

Above

Revivals from antiquity
Saint-Trophîme, Arles, west portal, circa 1180. The fluted columns of the portico frame statues of Jesus' disciples. The decoration belongs to the repertory of Roman architectural ornament.

Below

Classical perspective effects, Saint-Gilles-du-Gard, central portal, late twelfth century. The prominence of the central portal is ensured by columns carrying a projection of the entablature.

Soon after 1100, when the Romanesque style had attained its full maturity, sculpted and carved decoration began to pervade the entire façade of the church. Romanesque sculptors in this way elaborated remarkable monumental façades, which they based on models from classical antiquity, such as triumphal arches and city gates.

The entrance porch could easily be made to resemble a triumphal arch, as at Città Castellana, or a ciborium resting on columns, as at Modena, Cremona, Piacenza, or San Zeno in Verona. The base of the columns in such cases was frequently ornamented with a couchant lion holding its prey between its claws; the prey is generally a man, or a ram, stag or other animal. Such lions had a symbolic role as guardians of the sanctuary.

The influence of antiquity is also clear in superposed relief ornament. Romanesque sculptors reused items of classical sculpture, as we know from the Gallo-Roman lintel at Beaujeu. They also drew on classical sarcophagi in composing friezes, as is evident in the example at Nîmes cathedral. The western portal of Saint-Trophîme at Arles exhibits an architrave and frieze composition, designed in imitation of a colonnaded portico with statues between the columns. The monumental sculpted Romanesque façade did not reach full maturity until the late twelfth century.

The form and composition of the façade of Ripoll in Catalonia afford clear evidence of the triumphal aspect so characteristic of Romanesque façades. The portal is in the form of a triumphal arch and presents two superposed registers, emphasised by the tiering of the columns at the corners and by a continuous frieze. The blocks of stone are set one on top of another without mortar. The upper register shows Christ surrounded by angels, the symbols of the Evangelists John and Matthew, and the twenty-four elders of the Apocalypse. This is a Christian transformation of Roman iconographic programmes, whose function was to glorify the Emperor. Moreover, the statues of the Apostles Peter and Paul on the reveals are effectively in the round, and, from the shoulders down, constitute the bulk of the column. Yet they are not load-bearing; their function is not structural but iconographic.

This tendency is particularly clear in the monumental façade of Saint-Gilles-du-Gard. Its order is derived from those of Roman triumphal arches, with three portals set in a carefully judged array of columns and sculptures. The classicising aspect of the work is especially evident in the pilasters carrying sculptures, and in the portico constituted by columns and entablature. The tympanum of the central portal (a seventeenth-century copy of the Romanesque tympanum) shows a Christ in Majesty and the symbols of the evangelists; the tympana of the portals on either side show the Epiphany and the Crucifixion respectively. The façade of Saint-Gilles is a synthesis of the classical heritage, which the Romanesque sculptors placed at the service of the Church Triumphant.

An important centre of Romanesque sculpture: Moissac

Saint-Pierre, Moissac, detail from the east wall of the south porch, 1120–1135. This relief forms part of a frieze that represents the Childhood of Christ. Here we see the Flight into Egypt. The volumes of the figures, which are perfectly adapted to the very narrow architectural framing of the frieze, are typical of Romanesque carving.

Sculpture

This is a work about architecture, but it is difficult, in terms of the Romanesque, to separate architecture from the monumental sculpture that constituted, above all in the twelfth century, its prestigious outer garment. In the late eleventh century Romanesque art rediscovered classical sculpture. Artists began to reuse the Corinthian capital and adopted the monumentality of classical decorative schemes. And the principal directions taken by twelfth-century Romanesque sculpture gained a wider currency by their diffusion along the Santiago pilgrimage route. In France, the Languedoc was most influenced by the decoration at Toulouse. In Spain, the Romanesque sculpted decorations of *camino francés* churches are clearly related, notably those of Santiago de Compostela, San Isidoro in León, San Martín at Frómista, and Pamplona and Jaca cathedrals. To these could be added buildings outside the pilgrimage route, such as Santa María at Iguácel, San Juan de la Peña, the main chapel of the castle at Loarre, and the church of San Salvador at Nogal de las Huertas. The churches of Saint-Sernin at Toulouse and the abbey church of Saint-Pierre at Moissac, on the French side of the Pyrenees, complete this group. There is a clear decorative scheme common to three major contemporary buildings, those of Toulouse, León and Compostela. The sculptors of the collegiate church of León are thought to have drawn on a continuous tradition of decorative sculpture dating from the Spanish High Middle Ages, and those of Toulouse to have been inspired by the sculpture of late antiquity in the region.

Whatever the origin, these widely different centres all showed a pronounced taste for classical antiquity. They used a kind of rough-hewn Corinthian, and their decorative vocabulary included fleurons and palmettes. Acanthus leaves were often decorated with balls and pine cones. To this classical repertory a further motif was added: interlace. This form of decoration developed, in the fully mature Romanesque style, into a network of stems in clear relief on the base of the Corinthian capital.

Amidst these floral motifs there soon appeared animals, in most cases lions or birds treated in schematic fashion. They are purely decorative motifs, well adapted to the structure of the capital, whose architectural role they emphasise. The human figure was represented in similarly abstract fashion as it found its way back into sculpted decoration. The sculptors followed various models in their treatment of the human figure. At Moissac and Toulouse, objects in ivory or precious metals were imitated. This is particularly clear in the pillars of the cloister of Saint-Pierre at Moissac, and in the sculpted slabs from the workshop of Bernard Gilduin at Saint-Sernin. The figures are adapted to their architectural role by being placed in standing positions within an arcade. They are treated in very flat relief, in the manner of ivory reliquaries such as that still to be seen at San Isidoro in León. By contrast, in Jaca cathedral and at San Martín at Frómista, the artists were influenced by Roman sarcophagi. If photographs of the sides of one of the Frómista capitals are placed end to end, they form a composition copied from a Roman sarcophagus dating from the reign of Hadrian, and known to have come from Huzillos, some twenty kilometres from Frómista. The figures brandishing serpents that decorate certain of the capitals of the cathedral of Jaca are similarly inspired by Roman works. The ornamental sculpture of San Isidoro at León and of Santiago is based on Roman reliefs or sculpture in the round.

The earliest sculpted decoration appeared inside churches on capitals and abacuses, which the Romanesque sculptors incessantly enriched and diversified.

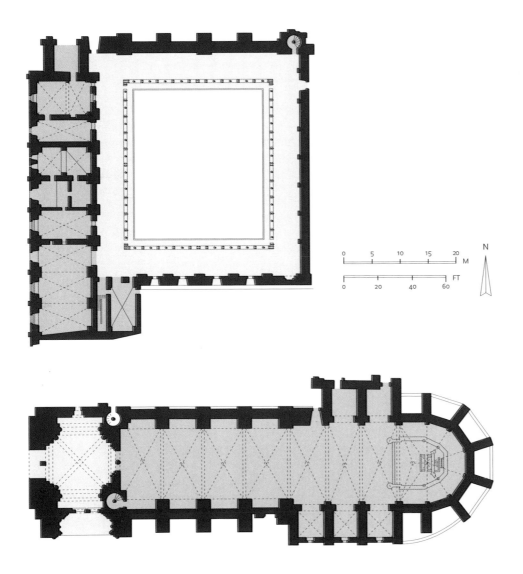

Layout of church and cloister
Saint-Pierre, Moissac, plan of the church and cloister, eleventh to twelfth century. The church is preceded by a tower porch comprising two storeys; the upper storey is accessible via spiral staircases. The four-bay nave is rib-vaulted. It opens on a wide chevet dating from the Gothic period with three oblong bays and a seven-section apse vaulted with prismatic rib vaults. The cloister is of traditional kind, with a porticoed courtyard around which the various monastic buildings are organised.

Left: Interwoven ornament
at Saint-Pierre, Moissac.
Right: Saint-Pierre, Moissac,
detail of the trumeau, 1120–1135.
The external face of the trumeau
is ornamented with three superposed pairs of lions, crossed or
affronted. Intricately woven
tracery is combined with exuberant decorative motifs. This riot
of ornament is reminiscent of
Assyrian art.

The 260 internal capitals in the collegiate church of Saint-Sernin in Toulouse placed at the springing of the semicircular arches present great stylistic continuity. Those of the lower parts and transepts are covered with a decoration including every kind of palmette. Those of the ambulatory are derived from Corinthian. The chevet, by contrast, offers historiated capitals continuing the style of the choir tribunes. Finally, in the outer aisles of the nave, the capitals are decorated exclusively with foliage. These sculpted elements can be dated. The sculptor Gayrard worked on them from the last quarter of the eleventh century until his death in 1118. A second sculptor, the above-mentioned Bernard Gilduin, executed an altar table that was consecrated in 1096; its sculpted forms are typical of a genre that belongs to the turn of that century. Similar works dating from the last decade of the eleventh century are found in Spain. At Saint-Sernin, the great importance accorded to the altar furniture is reminiscent of the sparkling precious metals and overall luxury of the interior of Santiago de Compostela. The oldest capitals are decorated with remarkable animal motifs strongly influenced by plant shapes.

In addition to the sculpture adorning the internal architecture and fittings, the outside of the church received ornamental sculpture, in particular the entrance: the façade, the portal and the tympanum. Here the spaces available to the Romanesque sculptors lent themselves to large-scale iconographic programmes. One of the oldest portals is the Porte des Comptes in the south transept of Saint-Sernin in Toulouse. Lacking a tympanum, the façade simply presents three figures of saints beneath arcades, including that of Saint Saturninus (Sernin), on a relatively small scale. Most historiated decoration was still, at this date, confined to the capitals, or placed in the splayed reveal of double windows. A major advance was the attempt, in the west portal of Jaca cathedral, to express a form of religious symbolism. But the protagonists of this composition are difficult to identify, and attempts to decipher it depend heavily on the many inscriptions.

The great Romanesque portal is a development of the years 1110–1115; examples are the Puerta Francigena and the Puerta de las Platerías at Santiago de Compostela, the Porte Miègeville at Saint-Sernin in Toulouse, and the Puerta del Cordero and Puerta del Perdón at San Isidoro in León. On either side of the archivolt there are generally two saints in high relief or in the round. At Saint-Sernin they are Saint Peter and Saint James; at San Isidoro, which conserves the relics of two saints, Isidore and Vincent, the statues of the saints feature in the Puerta del Cordero. The theme of the Ascension is represented in the Puerta del Perdón and in the Porte Miègeville. These two compositions exhibit considerable iconographic originality: angels on either side of Christ link arms to raise him into the sky. At León this scene is accompanied by a Descent from the Cross and a Resurrection that depicts the women at the empty tomb on Easter Day. In Toulouse, the Ascension carries over into the tympanum and lintel, and shows the apostles with their heads tilted back to watch Christ disappearing into the clouds. These compositions thus attained a language that is immediately comprehensible.

This new sophistication finds full expression in the tympanum of the Porte Miègeville at Toulouse. In the centre stands Christ, his feet on the ground and his raised arms held up by angels; his heavenward gaze suggests that he is about to rise into the air. He is surrounded by four angels, their gazes also turned towards the sky. The Ascension theme is thus clearly articulated. Moreover, the architect makes use of the architectural framework to distinguish the terrestrial from the celestial world; the apostles are confined to the lintel, while Christ stands at the centre of the tympanum.

The richest of these compositions are those of the cathedral at Santiago, where there were three portals. Two doors with semicircular arches of identical dimensions formed the Puerta Francigena, which has not survived. We know from documentary sources that Christ was represented in majesty, framed by the four Evangelists. The Garden of Eden and the fall of Adam and Eve were represented on the right-hand tympanum; the left-hand one showed the Expulsion from the Garden and the Annunciation. The south portal, the Puerta de las Platerías, is similarly composed of two doors with semicircular arches. A rectangle crowned by a cornice defines the architectural space of the composition. To the right are depicted the Passion and the Childhood of Christ and to the left the Temptation in the Desert. The west portal was also Romanesque, and showed the Transfiguration; it was replaced by the Pórtico de la Gloria in the late twelfth century. The Pórtico is organised around a central trumeau carrying a statue of Saint James. The Last Judgment and the Apocalypse are depicted on the tympanum. The sculpture is rich and abundant, and the influence of Gothic style already clear. These compositions exhibit a historiated, figurative decoration of great exuberance, sometimes overflowing from the tympanum and covering part of the façade. Figurative compositions are also found on the salomonic columns.

Cloisters too received sculptural ornament. The oldest example of historiated Romanesque in southern France is at Moissac. The date of construction is given by an inscription on the central pillar of the west gallery: 'In the year of the Incarnation of the Eternal Prince 1100, this cloister was completed, in the time of Abbot Ansquitil. Amen.' The porticoed galleries are composed of marble colonnettes, alternately single and coupled, capped by splendid sculpted capitals with geometrical, plant and animal motifs. Classical fleurons combined with a design of plant stems and foliated scrolls completely cover the two rows of leaves on the base of the capital. The very low relief gives the appearance of embroidery; this is particularly true of the capitals, whose bases are no longer rough-hewn Corinthian but cubic.

The historiated scenes illustrate the Redemption, the Fall, and the story of Cain and Abel. A small number show episodes from the Old Testament, with Isaac, Samson, David and Daniel. The Childhood and Life of Christ are frequently illustrated. By contrast, the Passion appears on only two capitals, with the Washing of the Feet and a double representation of the Cross. The Biblical sequence is completed by scenes from the Apocalypse. Finally, certain capitals show the martyrdom of saints (Saints Stephen, Lawrence, Saturninus, Fructuosus, and others) and miracles from the lives of Saints Benedict and Martin.

A reliquary of carved ivory
Beatitudes casket, ivory on wood, 15.2 x 18 x 11.9 cm, eleventh century. Angels and male figures with halos are standing under arcades, uttering the Benedictions from the Sermon on the Mount: blessed are the peacemakers (left), blessed are the merciful (centre), and blessed are the pure in heart (right). (Museo Arqueológico Nacional, Madrid)

A first step towards Gothic
Santiago de Compostela cathedral, relief from the Puerta de las Platerías, early twelfth century. This figure in very low relief is embedded in the left-hand buttress of the door. He is identifiable as David by the rebec that he played to combat the melancholy of King Saul. The crossed legs are similar to those of the figures of the nobles at Toulouse. The arrangement of the David, and of the figures embedded in the column to the right, prefigure the creation of column-statues.

One of the most distinctive features of the cloister is the marble slabs, sculpted in low relief, with which the brick pillars are faced. Figures of two apostles under arcades occupy each of the four corner pillars. The central pillar of the east gallery is faced with an effigy commemorating the first Cluniac abbot of Moissac, Durand de Bredons (1048–1072), who restored the spiritual and material life of the abbey. The prominent position accorded to the image of this saintly man is highly significant, affirming as it does the monks' desire to establish an ideal life, such as that lived by the Apostles after the Ascension. This in its turn illustrates the importance of the role that the monastic order sought to play in the Church.

The sculpted capitals of Moissac offer rich, harmonious compositions. The figures are of small dimensions, and stand out clearly on what is generally an extensive plain background. The detail is clear and abundant. Note that the historiated capitals are not arranged in continuous sequences: the episodes are scattered among the four galleries of the cloister. Generally, the sculptor has represented a single scene on each face of the capitals, which are double if the colonnette is a double one. But this framework is not rigorously respected, and some scenes overflow on to the next side. Others are linked by a common decorative or figurative motif.

Once the cloister of Moissac was finished, certain of the sculptors undertook a further series of capitals for the priory of La Daurade, an abbey near Toulouse belonging to Moissac. Work there was interrupted, then began again with a highly ambitious project involving twelve capitals, which were to show the story of the Passion and Resurrection, from the Washing of the Feet to Pentecost. Alas, this cloister was destroyed during the French Revolution. Surviving elements show that the Master of La Daurade grouped scenes from a single narrative on a single corbel. On one capital, for example, we find the Kiss of Judas, the Arrest and Judgment of Christ, the Flagellation, and the Carrying of the Cross. Many of the scenes unfold beneath arcades in which the column is sometimes omitted, to increase the space available. Others have a guilloche background, which, like the arcades, is reminiscent of ivory carving and silver- or goldwork. If the number of surviving examples is representative, historiated cloisters were rather rare in the first decades of the twelfth century. At Conques, for example, the cloister built by Abbot Bégon (1087–1107) features few such capitals.

These compositions illustrate how an iconography peculiar to the Romanesque cloister was emerging in the very late eleventh and very early twelfth centuries. Thenceforth, the association of architecture and sculpture in cloisters was inevitable, and this association soon extended to the whole of the mature Romanesque style. Sculpture pervaded capitals, façades, cloisters and the architecture of the church in general; it welcomed the faithful and outlined the essential elements of the Christian liturgy. The pilgrimage routes seem to have played an important part in the development of an iconographic programme. This was also the time when the tympanum came into use, and with it the possibility of creating a sculptural synthesis of the Christian doctrine: the Church's vision of the ordering of the world. Henceforth a façade lacking sculpted decoration was incomplete. The Romanesque sculptor placed his art at the service of God, working for the greater glory of God. He was greatly appreciated by the society of his time; though it is, for the most part, religious art that has survived, we know that sculptors also worked for rich lords who wished to embellish private residences.

Page 77
Galleries in which to meditate
Gerona Cathedral, cloister, second half of the twelfth century. The cloister is trapezoidal in plan. The galleries are spanned by heavy, continuous quadrant vaults, with the exception of the barrel-vaulted north gallery. A series of arcades resting on twin columns crowned with remarkable sculpted capitals lies between rectangular piers. The pillars are integrated into the structure by the columns at each of their corners; a historiated frieze runs around the pillars at capital height.

The Cloister

The cloister was for the exclusive use of the religious community and constituted a centre of monastic life. Generally situated alongside one of the aisles of the nave, in most cases the south aisle, it was a place of meditation and relaxation, and a passage leading to the various buildings used every day by the monks: the chapter house, dormitory, *scriptorium*, refectory, cellar, kitchen and so on. Certain rites, such as the washing of feet, might also take place there. Its square or trapezoidal form derived from the atriums found in Roman houses and later incorporated in the basilicas of late antiquity. This connection between the medieval cloister and the Roman atrium is particularly clear in the atrium of San Lorenzo in Milan, which possesses little rooms along its side that can be reached via staircases placed in two ante-rooms.

The cloisters of the eleventh century are not normally ornamented with sculpture, though some have capitals with stylised plant motifs. They are generally of irregular plan, and comprise four arcaded galleries of semicircular barrel vaults resting on masonry pillars. The cloister of Saint-Philibert at Tournus (1050) offers a more complex structure, with pillars flanked by colonnettes on two sides. The cloister of the cathedral of Besançon (1050–1060) and perhaps that of Saint-Guilhem-le-Désert (1060–1070) alternated thin colonnettes with quadrangular pillars.

Only over the course of the twelfth century did sculpture begin to cover cloister capitals and pillars. Moissac abbey has the oldest example (dated 1100) of a cloister with carved figurative decoration to have survived intact. It comprises four timber-roofed galleries opening on to the central space through arcades resting on marble colonnettes alternately single and paired. At the four corners and in the centre of each side stand quadrangular pillars. The great originality of this cloister is precisely these brick pillars, which are faced with marble slabs sculpted in low relief with figures of the Apostles depicted beneath arcades. The style draws on the example of ivory plaques and objects in precious metals. The historiated capitals illustrate the Old Testament, scenes from the Apocalypse, and the lives of the saints.

A considerable advance is marked by the capitals of the priory of La Daurade in Toulouse. In contrast with those at Moissac, they represent not isolated scenes but a continuous narrative; in this, they are analogous to illuminated Bibles in which a narrative is illustrated over several pages. Narrative continuity was enthusiastically adopted in the twelfth century, as witness the cloisters of Gerona, Sant Cugat del Vallès and Tarragona.

Above left
Harmonious cloisters
Sant Cugat del Vallès, cloister, late twelfth century. Four galleries are laid out on a 30 m square plan. They are spanned by a semicircular barrel vault in dressed stone. Each gallery comprises three sections of five arcades, set on twin columns crowned with sculpted capitals.

Below left
A later cloister
Saint-Trophîme, Arles, cloister, last third of twelfth century. The cloister has two Romanesque and two Gothic galleries. The arcades rest on twin columns with sculpted capitals.

Above right
Historiated capitals
Sant Cugat del Vallès, detail of a capital in the cloister. The capital forms an inverted pyramid. The corners are decorated with little towers, each of which has a conical roof with petal-shaped tiles. Beneath these is shown the Annunciation.

Page 79 above left
Embroidery in stone
Saint-Pierre, Moissac, detail of cloister capital, circa 1100 The capital is rough-hewn from a cube, and its entire surface covered in leaves and foliated scrolls. There is no undercutting and not an inch is left free. Of all the surviving Romanesque cloisters, that of Moissac is one of the most richly adorned.

Above right
The oldest historiated cloister
Saint-Pierre, Moissac, the cloister, circa 1100. The four galleries open on to the broad garth through arcades resting on alternating single and double colonettes. Massive pillars stand at each corner and in the middle of each arcade. The sculpted decoration of this cloister is the oldest historiated sequence, and shows the influence of ivory- and goldwork.

A fine medieval façade
Notre-Dame, Le Puy-en-Velay, cloister, second half of the twelfth century. Abutting the north aisle of the cathedral, the cloister is rectangular in plan. The four galleries are groin-vaulted. The arcades opening on to the garth rest on supports flanked by engaged columns. The abundant sculpted decoration on the capitals is complemented by the fine polychrome masonry of the walls.

Sturdy cloister galleries
Former cathedral Sainte-Eulalie, Elne, Roussillon, twelfth century. The cloister forms an irregular quadrilateral; the stone vaults are carried by intersecting ribs. Each gallery comprises four sections of three arcades divided by piers and supported by twin columns with sculpted capitals.

TOWN AND COUNTRY

Civic and Military Architecture

Page 81
The *urna* of Saint Domingo
Lid of the tomb, known as the *urna* of Saint Domingo, *émail brun*, circa 1150–1170, detail. An apostolic figure stands beneath an arcade set on columns with capitals and surmounted by architectural elements. (Monastery of Santo Domingo, Silos)

Ostentation in domestic architecture
Town house of the Granolhet family, Saint-Antonin, before 1155, detail of a pillar in the openwork of the window. This openwork is organised around three groups of three colonnettes, separated by pillars. That shown here displays an admirable ornamental sculpture of Adam and Eve. The decoration testifies to the desire of the emerging urban bourgeoisie to display their wealth.

Medieval towns generally grew up on the site of a classical town; there are numerous examples in Spain and France. And the classical urban plan was often respected. In the Mediterranean basin, the classical urban structure remained an essential component of the medieval town. Not so in the north, however; archaeology undertaken in the aftermath of the Second World War has provided a new insight into the workings of northern medieval cities. Country life continued to exist, of course; but we should be clear about the fact that, in the Romanesque era, urban life predominated.

The Town

Medieval towns featured a Jewish quarter. This was not invariably called a ghetto; the name differed from place to place and period to period. It was generally placed on the outskirts and had its own community facilities, such as a hospital, workshops, and so on. Most, but by no means all, Jews lived in the Jewish quarter. The Jewish quarter of Perpignan, Le Call, is a good example of this, though in fact it dates from the thirteenth century. In 1243 the Jewish inhabitants of the town were offered their own quarter. They could inhabit other quarters until 1251, the date at which Blanche, the Queen Regent of France, responding to the demands of the populace, confined them to the ghetto. In other towns, for example Carpentras, the process was reversed, and the Jews were released from their confinement, no doubt at a price. The fact that Jews spontaneously gathered in a specific quarter has often been explained by their need to be close to their religious buildings. The synagogue was the most important building in the Jewish quarter. We possess many documents describing French synagogues, but few have survived.

The discovery of a synagogue in Rouen in 1976 afforded a clearer notion of Jewish art of this time. The structure is similar to that of Norman palaces, and the synagogue was identified largely by the presence of *graffiti* on its walls and by its position. It dates from around 1100, and is rectangular in plan. The external walls are buttressed and exhibit rows of colonnettes. Light entered the lower room through four windows with a double-splay embrasure – a feature rarely found elsewhere in Normandy – and the upper storey was probably lit in the same way. The outside of the synagogue was magnificently decorated. Only the bases of the external sculpted decoration remain, but these provide an indication of the quality of the carving. The mixture of carved geometrical and plant motifs is similar to that of other contemporary Norman buildings, such as the church of Saint-Georges in Saint-Martin-de-Boscherville. The lack of internal decoration provided further confirmation of the function of the building.

Of public baths in Christian territory, the 'Arabic baths' at Gerona in Spain are the finest example to have survived. Completed about 1194, they are similar in plan to classical bath complexes, and thus to certain 'Turkish' baths in the West. The *frigidarium* presents an annular corridor with columns carrying the central drum; at the centre is an octagonal *piscina*.

There was considerable traffic around medieval towns. Road transport was increasing, thanks to more intelligent exploitation of horsepower; horses were now shoed and more lightly harnessed. The building of city gates and walls, and the creation and repair of roads, along with the building of bridges, counted among the prestigious large-scale urban works of the period. Roman bridges, too few and frequently in a state of disrepair, were replaced by new ones, whose piers at least were built in stone.

Shortly after 1042 a canon of Saint-Salvi described the building of the bridge at Albi. A bridge was demanded by the inhabitants of the town and nearby villages and castles and by the bishoprics of Nîmes, Cahors and Rodez; it was funded by Saint-Salvi's *allodium* (freehold) of the Tarn and by the ferry-toll. Bridges were also built at Châtellerault (over the Vienne, shortly before 1060), at Mâcon (before 1077), at Lyons (over the Saône, around 1077), and at Grenoble (1100). Bridge architecture became increasingly adventurous; examples include the bridges at Rouen (1144–1145), Avignon (Saint-Bénézet bridge, 1177–1185), its construction funded entirely by alms, and Narbonne, where in the early thirteenth century the Roman bridge was replaced by a new one. Increased tolls permitted the improvement of the road system. Famous architects, such as Mateo (the builder of the Pórtico de la Gloria at Santiago de Compostela) and Pedro Deustamben (at León) worked on the construction of roads and bridges.

The road system developed simultaneously with the creation of a network of parishes in the countryside. Between them, the highways and the administrative system enabled numerous contacts between town and country, gradually leading to interdependence.

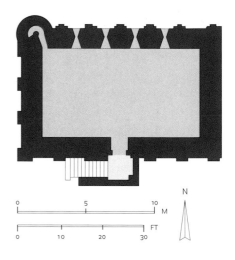

Synagogue architecture
Synagogue, Rouen, circa 1100, plan. It was a rectangular building reached by a staircase abutting the south wall. Light entered the lower level through four bays with double splay windows. The layout of the first floor is unknown to us. The very simple plan of this building has clear analogies with the houses of nobles during this period.

Page 84 above left

The synagogue: centre of the Jewish quarter

Synagogue, Rouen, circa 1100. The walls are reinforced on the outside by buttresses flanked by columns. The originality of the building consists in the double splay of the windows, a feature rarely found in the region. This is one of very few surviving examples of Jewish architecture in a medieval town.

Page 84 above right

Rich decoration

Synagogue, Rouen, detail of the carved base of a column. The decoration of the exterior of the synagogue comprised carving of a very high quality, as the bases of the colonnettes testify. These plant and geometrical motifs have affinities with other Norman monuments, such as Saint-Georges-de-Boscherville.

Above

A medieval public bathhouse

The so-called 'Arabic baths', Gerona, before 1194, exterior view with dome, restored. The dome rests on an octagonal drum set on eight colonnettes. This superstructure is carried by the eight slender columns surrounding the pool of the changing-room beneath. The Gerona bathhouse illustrates the structure of medieval Muslim baths.

Reminiscences of Roman *thermae*

'Arabic baths', Gerona, changing-room. The octagonal central pool is set under a baldaquin of eight columns with sculpted capitals. This first room leads through to the *frigidarium*, the *tepidarium* and finally the *caldarium*, which is directly connected to the building's heating system. With the exception of the bathhouse in Majorca, this complex is one of the few surviving example of its kind.

France

In the eleventh and twelfth centuries, new towns came into being. On the outskirts of existing towns, new market towns, some of which had their own walls, grew up around monasteries; Saint-Martin-des-Champs outside Paris or Saint-Martin outside Tours are examples of this tendency. Note, however, that cities could possess land outside the city wall. Villages, too, were sometimes walled. Neither the territorial nor the symbolic extent of the city was defined by its walls. Monasteries on the outskirts of a town were joined to it by broad converging streets, as at Charlieu or Saint-Denis, or were simply absorbed into the town, as at Aurillac or Figeac. Market towns sometimes grew up around isolated monasteries, such as Cluny, Saint-Denis, or Conques. But this was not inevitable; Saint-Michel-de-Cuxa, for example, remained isolated.

Other market towns emerged in the shadow of castle walls. These were very numerous in France, and their plans varied a great deal, since they had to follow the terrain around or beneath the castle. Castle and city were often built on the banks of a river, and this obviously influenced their layout, as we can see at Château-Thierry or Chinon. The town may encircle the castle, as at Montluçon or Gourdon, whether the latter is situated in the plain (Châteauroux) or on a plateau (Pau). The history of Caen is more complex; there, the two market towns of Saint-Jean and Saint-Pierre had existed since the eleventh century, each with its own parish church, and a further small town had grown up around the castle. The formation of towns under the castle walls took place in a variety of different ways.

Though towns grew rapidly in France during the eleventh and twelfth centuries, their rate of growth was notably inferior to that in Central Europe. Particularly in southern France, the phenomenon of *sauvetés* (townships founded by monasteries as sanctuaries for fugitives) meant that some townships were accorded safeguards and protection. A stretch of land of varying size was defined, and a charter obtained, through the intermediary of a military or religious order, authorising the

The urban bridge
Pont Valentré, Cahors, 1306–1355. This fortified bridge has affinities with Romanesque bridges in its solid stone piers carrying high defensive towers. Bridge building was one of the most prestigious forms of public works in the Middle Ages. This particularly well-preserved bridge is a fine example of medieval public architecture.

An isolated monastery
Saint-Michel-de-Cuxa, exterior, second half of the tenth century. This monastery is sited on the banks of the River Têt, which is now in the *département* of Pyrénées-Orientales, at the foot of Mont Canigou. Aid from the *contado* and the ever closer contacts between Rome and the Catalan church meant that its wealth grew steadily; its prestige as a religious centre continued throughout the Middle Ages. Despite the abbey's great renown, no town grew up around it.

construction of a village. Towns of this kind were generally laid out in one of two ways. One was a linear plan: the township developed along an axis (a road or street), and the church was placed at one end. Examples of this are Villefranche-sur-Cher and Sauveterre-de-Béarn. The other was a central plan, with the township built around the church, as at Couvertoirade and Beaumont-en-Argonne. The growth of cities continued throughout and after the twelfth century with *bastides*, settlements on a rectangular grid built around two axes at whose intersection was the central square; they were normally fortified. As early as 1114, the foundation of Montauban followed this plan.

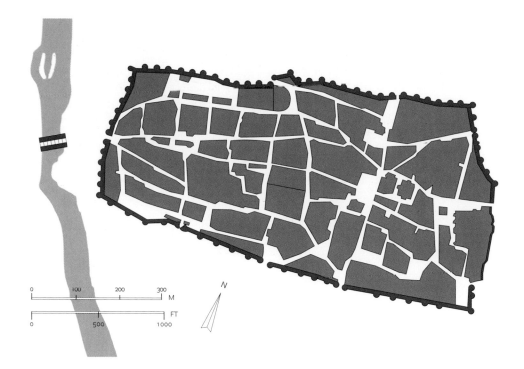

Iberian Peninsula

In the Iberian Peninsula, by contrast, towns are more diverse in kind and origin. This variety originated through the coexistence of Christian and Islamic civilisations. A new type of town made its appearance after the reconquest began in the eleventh century, when Islamic cities were transformed and adapted to the needs of Christian occupants. In the late eleventh and throughout the twelfth centuries, new cities proliferated in the Christian kingdoms in the north of the peninsula, often thanks to concessions and freedoms granted by the king. Towns sometimes arose where expanding village frontiers met. This was the process by which, starting in 1147, Salamanca came into existence. It seems that, in the mid-twelfth century, Segovia and Ávila too were collections of villages rather than towns.

At Ávila, the creation of an enclosed city resulted from the need for defensive walls. The town of Soria grew up around a frontier post between Castile and Aragon established in 1111. Alfonso I then promoted an influx of peasants to the city by according numerous privileges, intended to increase the population of this new and strategically important town. New towns grew up at strategic points to service the Santiago pilgrimage route, at Sahagún in 1085 and at Logroño in 1095. Older towns such as Burgos, Lorca, Burguete, Castrojeriz and Estella underwent structural modifications to adapt to the many new settlements arising along the Santiago route.

New towns on grid plans, like the *bastides*, made an early appearance in the Iberian Peninsula, at Sangüesa and Puente la Reina in Navarre, Briviesca in Castile, and Castellón and Villareal in eastern Spain. Vestiges of this medieval city architecture still survive in many towns: parts of the town named after the medieval parishes, an arcaded main street, a central square, and the original disposition of the suburbs.

On the Catalan coast, medieval towns often followed the Roman grid pattern. The old town in Barcelona is structured around two axes that meet at right angles in the rectangular main square, whose social role was similar to that of the classical forum. Tarragona and Gerona exemplify the creation of an ecclesiastical quarter around a cathedral built on a prominence, the result being a kind of town within the town.

The towers of the curtain wall
Ávila, detail of the fortified curtain wall, twelfth century. Made of stone and mortar, the towers are semicircular in form and integrated with the wall. The defensive purpose of the wall is emphasised by the crenellations. Castilian fortifications of this period differed from those of the rest of Europe in their use of round towers.

The town as collective fortress
Ávila, view of the curtain wall. The wall is 12 m high and studded, every 20 m, by semicircular towers that carry the parapet walk. The cathedral is integrated into the wall, and the houses of notables responsible for the town's defence back on to it.

Italy

Urban continuity in Italy can be said to have existed from the eleventh century on. Most of the large towns were in northern Italy. Some city walls were constructed as late as the thirteenth century, partly to meet military needs, partly because walls had a symbolic function, displaying the power, wealth and prerogatives of a city. But most cities preserved walls dating from late antiquity. Caserta Vecchia in Campania and San Gimignano in Tuscany are surviving examples of middle-sized medieval cities.

The square or rectangular plans of medieval towns often date from late antiquity. But cities were also built on concentric plans. By the thirteenth century, towns had generally assumed a circular shape around a quadrangular central square. The notion of the classical forum was conserved in this formula of a central square around which the important religious and administrative buildings were grouped. The great metropolises tended to be divided into quarters on the basis of either race or profession.

Venice was the single major city created in the Middle Ages, the other great cities having been in existence since antiquity. By contrast, many smaller cities affording all the possibilities of urban life grew up in the thirteenth century. There were hill towns and plains towns; of the latter, some grew spontaneously, in layers, such as the town of Aversa, near Naples, others on a linear plan, such as Castel San Pietro in Emilia, or on two intersecting axes, like Massa Lombarda.

In Rome, the larger and denser medieval city was superimposed on the ancient city and its traditions. The authority of the Vatican and the monastic orders, combined with the city's reputation as *caput mundi*, underlay certain transformations but

The heart of a medieval city
San Gimignano, general view. This Tuscan town has very broad main streets that divide it in two, separating the craft from the business quarters. Its most striking feature is the tower-houses. San Gimignano is a good example of a middle-sized medieval city.

The birth of a medieval island city
Venice, aerial view. The town came into being as successive islands were inhabited, and its layout was determined by its natural topography. The central artery was the Merceria, running between the piazza San Marco and the Rialto bridge. Public monuments were constructed: the Palace of the Doges, the Arsenal for the city's fleet, and the warehouses for trade. Venice was the only great Italian city to come into being during the Middle Ages; all the others are of Roman origin.

permitted other elements to survive unchanged. The twelfth century was a period of renaissance; urban development and construction were at their height. Throughout the century, Rome continued to enjoy its legendary status in Western Christendom. New churches were built, and new quarters constructed between Old Saint Peter's and the Castel Sant'Angelo. The Capitoline Hill, with its view over the forum, was again inhabited. The topography of the city had remained unchanged, and consequently the Roman walls that surrounded it survived.

The plan of thirteenth-century Rome is known to us from two versions of a single original. The city was oriented to the east and surrounded by an elliptical wall punctuated with towers. Within the walls were the Tiber, the island, the seven hills of the left bank and the Janiculum. The monuments and streets are indicated on the plan; the Castel Sant'Angelo, Pantheon and Colosseum are clearly marked. A narrow porticoed street led from San Giovanni Laterano to the Colosseum. Houses generally had porticoes at street level, with architraves and capitals in the twelfth-century style. Classical *spolia* were reused throughout the city, a practice exemplified in the early twelfth-century Casa di Crescenzio, which stands between the Capitoline and the Tiber.

England

The rise of urban living in England dates from the Norman Conquest in 1066, when many towns arose in the shelter of monasteries and castles. Here too towns were generally on either a longitudinal or a concentric plan, but the latter, which we find at Old Sarum (near modern Salisbury), was much less common. Oxford is an example of a market place being established on the main street, and the street then being widened to accommodate it. The monastic towns of Peterborough and Bury St Edmunds illustrate the juxtaposition of monastery and town. The feudal town of Ludlow exemplifies the longitudinal plan, with the castle at one end and the church at the other. Bristol, like Durham, was sited within the bend of a river. In small towns built where roads crossed (Carfax towns, such as Oxford), the market place was the most important feature. In towns with a radial plan, façades could be built not only on the market place itself but on the roads leading to it, and this proved a popular arrangement.

The richly ornamented façade of a palace
Estella, Palacio de los Reyes de Navarra, also known as Palacio de los Duques de Granada, about 1200. The south façade originally presented a ground floor and first storey only, to which a second storey and tower were added. Four large arches give access to a vestibule. Above them four windows are decorated with arcades. The rows of modillions and the columns set on sculpted capitals now frame the building, but originally supported the roof structure.

An episcopal palace

The bishop's palace, Auxerre, twelfth century. The palace stands alongside the cathedral. It comprises a large two-storey room with an adjoining chapel. The gallery is built on the old wall of the Gallo-Roman city. Few such buildings have survived; Auxerre's is essential to the study of episcopal palaces, which were constructed alongside or actually on city walls, and constituted part of the city's defences.

A prestigious gallery

The bishop's palace, Auxerre, detail of the gallery. Hugues de Montaigu embellished the palace with a loggia offering views over the River Yonne into the countryside. The gallery is 22 m long. The arcade is decorated with relief ball mouldings and rests on columns with sculpted capitals. The rich ornamentation is completed by the modillions at the cornice, and is typical of episcopal palaces.

Urban Civic Architecture

The abbot's palace at Pomposa in Italy, the Palazzo della Ragione ('Palace of Reason'), is a particularly fine example of prestigious civic architecture, most notably in its façade. The two levels of superposed arcades and the hollows in the façade impart an extraordinary sense of depth to the wall.

However, a new style was soon to become established in Italian town halls. The Palazzo della Ragione is not typical of this; it more closely resembles the palaces and houses of Venice. The use of brick for the walls and marble for the columns and capitals is one of the characteristics of the Venetian lagoon. The sobriety of the atrium, with its wide central opening at ground-floor level flanked by slightly lower lateral galleries, and the continuous galleried loggia of the first floor, are clear evidence that the building dates from the eleventh century. Its current aspect is the result of a restoration that returned it to its original appearance, removing the modifications begun by Abbot Bonaccorso in 1396.

In medieval Romanesque architecture, particular care was lavished on palace exteriors, even where there was no sculpted decoration or architectural ornament.

A relatively plain palace façade
Palazzo della Ragione, Pomposa, Italy, eleventh century, restored façade. The palace is preceded by an atrium, which is reached through a wide semicircular arch. The façade is decorated with two registers of arcades resting on slender columns interspersed with masonry pillars. Blind oculi animate the spandrels of the arcade. The overall effect is of sober elegance, enhanced by the unusual combination of brick walls with marble columns.

An Imperial chapel
Chapel of Sankt Ulrich in the Imperial palace of Goslar, early twelfth century. Goslar in Lower Saxony was an Imperial Diet town, where a palace with two chapels was built to accommodate the travelling Emperor. The chapel of Sankt Ulrich has two storeys, which form an impressive open space at the crossing.

The tomb of an Emperor
Chapel of Sankt Ulrich, view from the second storey into the crossing. The ground floor is in the form of a Greek cross, changing to an octagon in the second storey. In the crossing stands the tomb of Henry III; only his heart rests here.

A palace for the Emperor

Imperial palace, Goslar, circa 1150. The building as a whole exhibits the structure required of imperial architecture, concentrating in a single block the different functions of the palace. It was over-restored in 1873 and again in the twentieth century.

A form of sacred architecture

Imperial palace, Goslar, plan. The palace symbolised the Divine City and the Palace of the Lord.

1 Twelfth-century living quarters and courtyard
2 Reception hall
3 Living quarters
4 Atrium of the chapel
5 Chapel of the Virgin, reconstructed plan

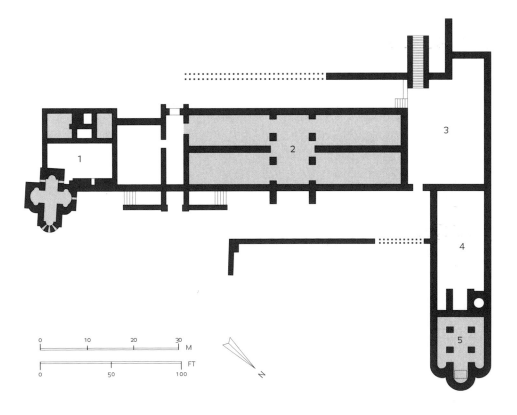

This is clearly the case with the Pfalz, the Imperial palace at Goslar, in Germany. Over and beyond the formal articulation of the palace, there is always an intention to emphasise its monumental volumes and its public presence. The urban imperial or baronial palace is marked by its ostentation, and can generally be identified by the characteristic open gallery on the façade. The palaces shown in the Bayeux tapestry have two floors; their prestige is declared by a row of arcades. The Wartburg (1157–1165) near the town of Eisenach in Thuringia is a little later. It is of very solid appearance, particularly in the wings and lower floors. The great hall usual in a palace is often divided into two aisles by a row of columns; these sometimes alternate with piers. Such internal rhythms find expression in the façades of the German palaces at Eisenach, Bad Wimpfen and Münzenberg. Goslar is a representative of the fortified princely palaces of Carolingian tradition.

Private town residences became increasingly common as the urban bourgeoisie prospered. They were generally tall buildings with cellars. External decoration was generally confined to the façade; bourgeois, feudal lord and churchman competed to create or own the finest example. The façades of private residences imitated those of palaces. A large portal occupied the ground floor; the openings were generally double windows with pointed or semicircular arches often protected by a discharging arch on the *piano nobile*. And, of course, there was rich decoration in the form of capitals, bases, tympana and reliefs. The internal layout of these buildings was primarily functional. The basement floor was generally rectangular in plan, sometimes with intermediate pillars; the ground floor was open and could be used as a warehouse or shop; finally, the first floor (and second, if there was one) provided for social and private life. The walls were built of stone, and adorned with murals and tapestries.

Few examples of private Romanesque residences have survived. The town house at Saint-Antonin in Tarn-et-Garonne is quite exceptional in having a three-storey elevation. It was commissioned in the twelfth century by a rich bourgeois family, the Granolhet: anxious to assert their status, they had this impressive building constructed on the west side of the place de l'Hôtel de Ville. In 1175 Raymond V, count of Toulouse, stayed there, and in the fourteenth century it became the seat of the town's consulate. The building consists of a residence abutting a tower. The façade of the residence proper displays three pointed arcades, above which is openwork incorporating three sets of three colonnettes; these are separated by pillars bearing superlative carvings of Adam and Eve and the Judgment of Solomon. Openwork allows light into the great reception room. On the top floor are three double bays with semicircular arches, which light the private rooms of the house. Originally, the façade was ornamented with faience, though this has long since disappeared.

The tower was a symbol of power often used by nobles and bourgeoisie in, for example, Toulouse. The Romanesque house at Cluny, that of Dol-de-Bretagne and the so-called Pavillon d'Adélaïde at Burlats are among the few surviving examples of private architecture from the Romanesque period. Like the palaces of the overlords, those of abbots and bishops had more than one floor.

In England, the private architecture of the eleventh and twelfth centuries followed a similar path. The Romanesque house in Christchurch, Dorset, is a two-storey residence incorporated into the castle; it originally had a timber roof. The ground floor, which has suffered much and been much restored, perhaps contained the servants' quarters. An internal staircase led up to the first floor, which was lit by large windows. From the mid-twelfth century, large Jewish houses were similar to those built in mainland Europe. Examples are Moyses Hall at Bury St Edmunds, the Jew's House and Music House in Norwich and the Jew's House and Aaron in Lincoln. These residences illustrate the wealth of the powerful Jewish bourgeoisie, who

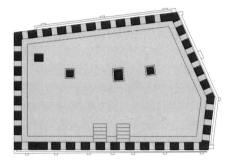

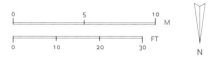

A Romanesque Council Hall
The Domus Municipalis or Council Hall, Bragança, late twelfth century, plan. The building is on an irregular trapezoidal plan. It is divided in two longitudinally; on the south side is a broad staircase giving access to the first floor. A stone bench runs entirely around the assembly hall. It is a perfect example of twelfth-century Portuguese civic architecture.

A solid building

Domus Municipalis, Bragança. The meeting hall is set over a large, vaulted cistern and lit by thirty-eight windows with semicircular arches separated by sturdy pillars. Above them, the sculpted modillions support the cornice on which the roof structure rests. These sculptural details do not detract from the impression of monumentality.

built sumptuous houses for themselves. The house built by the eminent Richard of Leicester in Southampton in the early thirteenth century is a further example.

Surviving examples of private urban architecture are so few that a regional study cannot be attempted. Among public buildings, the façade of the Casa de la Paeria de Lleida (Lérida), which has been heavily restored, foreshadows the great Gothic façades of the town's administrative buildings. The Domus Municipalis or Council Hall at Bragança (Portugal) dates from the late twelfth or early thirteenth century and is built over a large, vaulted cistern. Meetings for the Senate were held in its large hall lit by windows with semicircular arches.

Rural Architecture

Our knowledge of the rural habitat of Western Europe owes much to the excavations at Wharram Percy in Yorkshire. There, a group of dwellings grew up around the seigneurial manor in the late twelfth century (1186–1188). The church, which had undergone several reconstructions since the eighth century, stood at one end of the village. The manor house, built in stone, was the noblest representative of this village architecture. The houses surrounding it were rectangular in plan, with a lower part for animals; they occupied quadrangular enclosures.

Towards the middle of the thirteenth century, wood gave way to stone in the building of houses. Gomeldon, in Wiltshire, illustrates the transition from the mixed house (shared with animals) to the farm composed of a number of buildings set around a closed courtyard. This took place between the twelfth and fourteenth centuries. The only houses of which traces remain from the early twelfth century are mixed houses with a cruck-frame. This type of building existed in several parts of the Continent; many were still to be found in Brittany not so long ago. At Pen er Malo at Guidel (Morbihan), mixed oval-plan houses dating from the mid-twelfth century have been found.

The decline of the mixed house marks an advance in agricultural technique; it also testifies to the improvement in the financial standing of peasants. Though rural building was mostly in wood or stone, cob was also used; this is a mixture of straw, clay and pebbles made up into thick walls, which were then whitewashed. One of the buildings of the late twelfth to early thirteenth centuries brought to light during the excavations at Wallingford Castle in Oxfordshire was constructed of cob. It had three rooms, each of them with a hearth.

Architecture at one with the landscape
Castle, Almourol. Built in 1171 on an islet in the River Tagus, this fortress has a crenellated curtain wall and a central keep. Its purpose was to command the ford and resist Muslim attacks. It is one of the most impressive examples of medieval military architecture.

The fortified medieval castle
Château-Gaillard, Les Andelys,
1196–1198. Built on the summit
of a rocky spur, the castle has an
elliptical curtain wall and a
four-storey cylindrical keep.
A drawbridge protects the
monumental entrance portal.
Château-Gaillard is a fine example
of the fortress with keep of the
late twelfth century.

Military Architecture

The castle played an important social role during the Romanesque period; along with monasteries and parish churches, it provided a focus for other dwellings and thus contributed to the transformation of the rural landscape. The castle was primarily defensive in function. But it was also the dwelling of the feudal overlord. Its structure had therefore to fulfil the requirements of residence and reception. As a seat of administration or as an agricultural centre, it might have other functions too; life was organised around the castle. Castles were often constructed at the lord's request. By the twelfth century the right to construct was eagerly contested, sometimes giving rise to conflict and insubordination. Implementing the suzerain's right to fortify often required the exercise of military force. More and more castles were built; they became a symbol of seigneurial power.

The wealth of the castle governor often derived from agriculture. The reorganisation of local administration conferred real power on him. A group of knights was attached to the castle; they lived locally, and took part in military expeditions. These elements consolidated the feudal structure.

Castles were built at strategic sites. As they were required both to defend the lands of the suzerain and to assert his power, fortified sites were sometimes abandoned when changes in the regional social structure made other sites more suitable. Groups of castles are sometimes found.

The dwellings that grew up around castles were often the kernel from which a village or market town arose. Sometimes it is unclear which came first, castle or village. The castle often replaced a farm building and therefore arose at the centre of an agricultural holding. Proximity to a monastery was sometimes thought desirable. Castles were not always built on the site of an abandoned town; when they were built in isolated and underpopulated places, the preparation of the ground and the organisation of land use presented immense difficulties.

The form, structure and function of castles varied from region to region. The site chosen for a residence was of considerable importance in frontier zones. Territories were not constituted by linear borders, but by the siting of the fortresses from which feudal lords could launch attacks and ensure the protection of the region. The frontier castle was one of the most important symbols of the power of a sovereign relative to his enemies and neighbours. Other castles controlled land-routes and were enriched by tolls demanded as payment for right of passage across the feudal lord's holdings.

Defending a castle was no easy matter. Attacks could take the form of scaling the walls, ballistics and siege-towers. Mining or surface impact might effect a breach in the curtain wall. Siege was a standard tactic, and the fortress had to be capable of long periods of autonomy. A deep moat was the most effective counter to attack by scaling of the walls. The central keep was surrounded by a series of baileys, all of which had to be breached before the keep could be assailed. Projecting towers defended the curtain walls; angle towers offered a wide radius of defensive fire. Gates were few and strongly protected. The walls were generally of medium-sized stonework, and contained loopholes; they were crowned by a crenellated parapet with machicolation. The walls of towers and keeps in particular were reinforced at their bases by the construction of a scarp.

Gautier de Thérouanne described the castle at 'Merchem' (possibly Merkem, near Dixmunde, Belgium) in Flanders in the years 1100–1130: 'By the side of the church graveyard there stood a high tower, which one can call castle or fortress, built many years before by the lords in the manner of the region; for, in this part of the country, it is the custom of the rich and noble to pile up a huge motte of earth, as high as they can make it, and to dig a moat around it, as wide and deep as possible; to enclose the plateau at the summit of the motte with a palisade of planks assembled in extremely solid fashion to form a rampart, to which are added, wherever possible, a certain number of towers. Within this wall, they construct a residence, or rather a fortress, at the centre; this must command the entire perimeter. It is arranged in such a fashion that the entrance to the castle is accessible only by a bridge which rises from the counterscarp of the moat in a gentle slope, held up at intervals by double or even triple posts. Its slope is calculated in such a way that, having crossed the moat, it meets the crest of the palisade, and this point is the threshold of the gate.' This is a precise definition of the Romanesque motte and keep.

The motte first appeared in Western Europe between the Rhine and the Loire in the early eleventh century. The oldest mottes in England are those built by Norman immigrants following the Conquest. Mottes are not found in the Iberian Peninsula. The most common form was a truncated cone, but in the following century quadrilaterals with rounded corners became increasingly common. Access to the motte was via a gangway resting on large posts, which linked the area outside the moat to the motte's summit. Sometimes two or three mottes were connected for reasons of kinship between the castle owners or simply for better defence.

A continuous line of development links the primitive motte of the tenth century to the fortress of the mid-thirteenth century. The earliest mottes were built on natural prominences; those on plains were first built in the early thirteenth century. Those constructed on hilltops were high and circular, leaving only a small area at the summit; their moats were dry and extremely deep. Mottes built on spurs of land were adapted to the lie of the land; those on slopes tended to be oval. A third type of motte was that built on the steep edge of a plateau in order to dominate a valley. Most of the plains type were rectangular or circular. The bailey was then adapted to the lie of the land, with the lowest section of the motte linked to the rampart and the shallowest part of the moat.

Excavations of the chapel motte at Doué-la-Fontaine have made it possible to

The Pfalz at Wimpfen
The so-called 'Blue Tower', early thirteenth century. At Wimpfen the Hohenstaufen dynasty built their greatest Imperial palace. This tower, built in a regional, blue-coloured stone, defended the palace on the side of the city, where there was no natural protection by a steep slope.

Left

A residential keep
The keep at Houdan, twelfth century. This quadrangular keep has four projecting turrets. It is 30 m high and 15 m wide, with walls 3.5 m thick. The ground floor comprises a single room 8 m square. The living quarters are on the first floor, where the towers are cut away internally to form part of the living space, and on the second floor. It is a typical example of the residential fortresses that developed during the twelfth century.

Right

The 'Red Tower'
On the east end of the palace at Wimpfen stands this tower built from cubic blocks of sandstone and tufa. In case of siege, it probably was the ultimate place of refuge for the king. The second storey contains a living room with fire place and toilet.

reconstruct the development of a medieval fortified site. The residential *aula* or hall of the first third of the tenth century was rebuilt in stone after it was burnt down shortly before 950. Here we witness the birth of the monumental keep. The walls of the rectangular hall (which thus became a cellar) were raised and the doors positioned at a height of five metres. The joists underpinning the new floor were carried on retaining posts, and the new storey was lit by windows.

Other noble residences, such as that at Langeais, adopted this plan in the mid-tenth century. Finally, in the first half of the eleventh century, the two lower storeys of the keep at Doué-la-Fontaine were surrounded by a deep layer of earth and the upper parts raised still further; the keep had thus been 'enmotted'.

During the tenth century, both stone and wooden keeps were found in the central Loire and the Anjou regions. The culmination of the stone keep was attained during the eleventh century, as we can see from those at Langeais, Vendôme and Montbazon. Until the late twelfth century, the quadrangular keep was the most common form; examples include Gisors and Houdan. It stood either on its own or in the midst of a fortress. Various defensive outworks might surround it. Three sets of walls might be built; the first surrounding the outer bailey, the barns and the dependencies; the second surrounding the chapel, the storehouses and the garrison quarters; and a third, the *chemise*, protecting the keep-residence.

The great, square Norman keeps are similar to those in England. Those of Caen, Arques and Falaise date from about 1115. Cylindrical or truncated pyramidal towers rising above the residential keep are found in the castles of Foix, Dax and Pau in southwest France, and at Paris and Provins. From the thirteenth century on, military construction in the Languedoc and Aude caught up with these advances, as Peyrepertuse, Aguilar and Quéribus testify.

The buttressed keep spread throughout England and the west of France. Openings were confined to the upper storeys, and the gate opened out from the first or second storey and was at least five metres above the ground. Each storey comprised a single room. The lowest levels were vaulted and had no doors or windows; access was through a trapdoor in the summit of the vault. The first storey was a reception area, while the living quarters as such were on the second storey. Loches exemplifies this arrangement. In due course, the circular or polygonal keep was preferred, for its wider radius of fire and superior defensive qualities.

The chronicler Lambert d'Ardres described a fortification built around 1099 by Arnoul, the suzerain of Ardres in the Pas-de-Calais. On the summit of the motte was built 'a wooden residence, a masterpiece of woodwork, more beautiful than any other castle in Flanders. The builder was a carpenter from Bourbourg named Lodewick, who may be compared to Daedalus for his industry; his work was a veritable labyrinth, in which were piled cellars, chamber upon chamber, corridor on corridor, with attics built directly upon cellars, and a chapel placed right at the top, on the east side.

The building formed three storeys, whose aerial floors were separated by vast distances. The first floor was at ground level. There were storerooms for the various harvests and for the castle's supplies of hampers, barrels, tuns and other utensils of this kind. On the second floor, the living quarters where the whole household met, were little rooms for the pantlers and cup-bearers, and the large bed-chamber in which the lord and his wife slept. Next to this stood the privy of the young ladies and the children's room or bedroom. The great chamber also had access through a concealed door to another recess, where a fire was lit morning and evening, for use when someone was ill or being bled, or to keep children warm while they were at the breast. The kitchen was fitted on to the outside of this storey, and in itself formed two storeys.

On the lower level were kept (separately) pigs, geese, capons and poultry, of which there was always a sufficient supply; above them were kept the casks and there, too, lived the kitchen assistants. Here were prepared the delicate repasts set before the masters and the food of the servants.

The upper storey of the castle was divided by beams into several different levels, each with their own access. There the sons and daughters of the lord slept, the former when they wished, and the latter regularly; there too slept the watchmen and sergeant assigned to the castle guard. Many staircases and corridors were

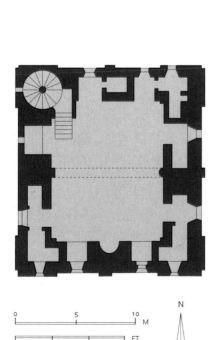

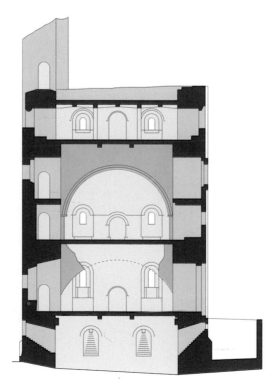

A residential keep
Castle Hedingham, Essex, circa 1130–1140, section and plan of the castle. Access to the four storeys is by stair-turret. The lowest floor was particularly vulnerable to attack, and its windows, with their semicircular arches, are narrow compared with those of the other storeys. Some of the latter are double windows surmounted by a triple archivolt. This is one of the most monumental keeps built in the aftermath of the Norman Conquest.

A fortified city

Carcassonne, the walls, late thirteenth century. This *cité comtale* (seat of a count) is protected by two curtain walls: the outside wall is 10 m high, the inner 14 m. Each has a parapet walk, battlements and machicolation. There are many towers of varying shapes: round, square and semicircular. The castle itself lies within the inner wall.

needed to go from one storey or room to another, either from the residential area to the kitchen or loggia (well-named, since it is intended for the pleasure of conversation, and takes its name from *logos*, discourse), or, finally, from the gallery to the chapel, whose carved and painted decoration made it comparable to Solomon's tabernacle.' This description could be applied to the internal organisation of any kind of keep.

Military and residential functions
Château Comtal, Carcassonne, twelfth to thirteenth century. The castle backs on to the inner curtain wall. It is a double residential block, approximately rectangular in plan, with its own curtain wall, separated from the town by a wide moat. At its centre stand two towers, the 'big' and 'small' keeps. The height of these was increased during the thirteenth century, as was that of the residential block, while a great hall was built along the south curtain wall.

Imposing fortifications
Carcassonne, structure of castle and curtain walls. There is a double line of fortifications, the outer some 1500 m long, the inner around 1200 m in length. The two walls enclose an area of 8 hectares. The external wall dates from the late thirteenth century. The inner wall is of uncertain date, but was probably built between the fourth and sixth centuries.
1 Castle (1230–1240)
2 Barbican
3 Outer wall

A masterpiece of military architecture

Carcassonne, general view of the upper town. Classified as a World Heritage Site, the fortified city is set on an escarpment, dominating the market town below. It survived the crusade against the Cathars in the thirteenth century, the attack of Simon de Montfort, and the conquest of the South by the North. Heavily restored by Viollet-le-Duc, Carcassonne is the most complete surviving complex of medieval fortifications.

Urban and Rural Fortification

In the Romanesque period, towns still sheltered behind Roman walls, which they consolidated or rebuilt. Walls and gates helped to define the city centre and were carefully maintained. The most representative of the surviving city walls in France are those of Carcassonne, Laon, Provins and Vitré. The castle at Carcassonne is quadrangular in plan; the double perimeter wall can be dated to the first quarter of the thirteenth century, and was built over a Roman wall. The much-rebuilt Mâchicoulis building at Le Puy probably dates from the thirteenth century, and is a well-preserved example of medieval fortification.

The walls around rural settlements consisted of an earth scarp and a moat. Some large, some small, they were built everywhere in France except the south. Among the largest are circular walls, with ramparts and moats like those around a motte; these were undoubtedly built for purposes of defence. There were also smaller agricultural enclosures that protected estates. From the twelfth century on, villages too tended to be fortified, and thus took responsibility for their own defence, no longer relying on the castle. In the thirteenth century, fortified farmhouses began to be transformed into fortified lordly residences and agricultural centres.

Churches and monasteries too were fortified from the twelfth century on, in particular in southern France. Such defensive works generally formed part of the original design. Some churches, many of which survive, were real fortresses; the tower was a veritable keep, and the walls were equipped with scarps, loopholes and machicolation. Churches might also be included within a larger system of fortification.

The British Isles

Residential keeps, such as are found in western France, proliferated throughout England after the Norman Conquest. The keeps at Christchurch in Dorset and Richmond in Yorkshire are classic examples. By contrast, Chepstow is a residential building designed to resist attacks. Above the cellar, there are two rooms, the first of which has a door and small windows, while the second is divided up into chambers. Some members of the nobility refused to build keeps where the site was already well protected, as at Westminster. Yet the fashion for keeps spread rapidly. The White Tower of the Tower of London is one of the most sophisticated examples, combining comfort with formidable defences. It was constructed during the last two decades of the eleventh century by William the Conqueror, who thus reinforced his London castle. From the outside it presents a strikingly symmetrical set of openings. It consists of a ground floor and two upper storeys, and is 35 m long and 30 m wide; the main body of the tower is 27 m high. The chapel, whose projecting semicircular apse is visible to the south-east, confirms that the keep also served as a palace. To the north-east there is a staircase tower. A peripheral corridor runs round the outside of the large halls. In Essex, the keep of Colchester Castle is more or less contemporary and shares this layout, though on a larger scale.

These two keeps were the model for other English castles, and were imitated on a larger scale in other royal fortresses. Examples include Norwich (1096–1145), Rochester (around 1130), Scarborough (1159–1168), Newcastle (1172–1177) and Dover (1180–1190). The royal fortresses were in turn imitated by the great nobles: by the Earl of Oxford at Castle Hedingham, in Essex; the Earls of Sussex at Rising in Norfolk (c. 1130–1140); the Clintons at Kenilworth in Warwickshire (c. 1150–1170) and in the middle of the century by the Earl of Huntingdon at Bamburgh in Northumberland. They constitute a homogeneous series; massive in structure, quadrangular in plan and less than 25 m high, they generally possessed one or two outbuildings connected to the keep at first-floor level. Flat buttresses strengthen the walls. A chapel completes the complex. The great hall of the keep at Rochester is a good example of the elegance of these fortresses and the care lavished on their decoration.

In Ireland, contact with England ensured that the development of military architecture followed a similar path after the Norman Conquest. The motte was the main type of fortification used after 1169. This was facilitated by the large number of motte-like constructions already in existence. The Normans made use of these, for example, at Knowth and Meath. Mottes tended to be circular from the late twelfth century on. Such earthen ramparts were often built on natural eminences in order to command the area around (as at Louth and Faughart), in frontier zones (such as Westmeath and Antrim), or on flat sites where they protected agricultural areas (as at Down and Dromore). The buildings on the summit were generally wooden. The great period for the building of fortifications in Ireland was 1170–1230.

Iberian Peninsula

In Romanesque Spain, new military construction was linked to reconquest of Muslim possessions and repopulation by Christian Spaniards. In Aragon and Catalonia a process of military and agricultural colonisation went on continuously, from the late tenth century to the end of the eleventh century and even into the early twelfth century. In the first phase of reconquest, defensive works were built to protect areas of recent agricultural development in the border zones. This defensive aspect was further emphasised in the late tenth and early eleventh centuries after the expeditions of Al Mansur, military commander of Córdoba.

The most widely copied model was that of a tower, which might have an adjoining chapel and perimeter walls. Catalonia, alone in Europe at this stage, preferred the round tower, though rectangular fortresses are also found. Tower and chapel were built in mortared rubble masonry, and outbuildings in dry stone. The

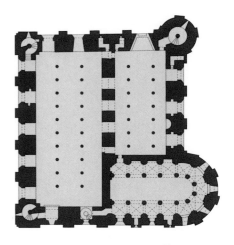

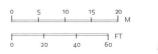

English military architecture
The White Tower (Tower of London), 1078–1097, plan. A three-storey tower, it comprises two rectangular halls and a chapel whose apse forms a projection to the south-east of the keep. To the north-east, a turret protects the staircase. This is one of the most successful examples of military architecture in Britain, combining defensive strength with comfortable living conditions.

Page 109
External decoration
The White Tower, London, detail of the façade. The defensive aspect of the tower is clear in the massive buttresses and the battlements by which the walls are topped. But the surfaces of the walls are animated by elegant blind arcades and double windows. Here is evidence of the care taken with the decoration of residential keeps.

residential keep made its first appearances in the late eleventh century in Aragon and the domain of Arnau Mir de Tost at Llordà.

A whole series of castles was built along the frontiers of Aragon. Most of them comprised a single rectangular, pentagonal or hexagonal tower with a rather under-developed perimeter wall. Within the walls were a variety of buildings, including chapels, cisterns and wells. The most celebrated of these castles is at Loarre, which was built at over 1000 m above sea-level and includes a well-known church. A sig-nificant part of the castle complex is contemporary with the first southern Romanesque. The buildings stand within a bailey, with the imposing keep – more than 22 m high – at their centre. Its gate was on the fifth of its six storeys. The castle itself was probably built simultaneously with the reconstruction of the chapel at the end of the twelfth century. The monastery of Loarre was founded in 1072; it too is fortified, and forms, with its surrounding village, a fine example of Romanesque military architecture.

The fortresses of Castellar and Montearagón were transformed, after the union of Aragon and Castile, into entrenched military camps designed to shelter entire armies for the duration of the sieges of Huesca and Saragossa.

In Castile, we find some Romanesque keeps identical to those in France. The oldest part of the so-called Torre de Doña Urraca at Covarrubias can be dated to the tenth century. It is 15 m long, 8 m wide and 18 m high; its internal layout resembles those of certain northern keeps. In Spain, as in France, the function of the keep as palace was an important one.

The symbolic fortress of Aragon
Loarre, eleventh–twelfth century, partial view of castle, keep and chapel. Loarre has a six-storey keep attaining 22 m in height; the entrance is on the fifth storey. Within the curtain wall stands the chapel, which was reconstructed in the twelfth century. Loarre offers precious evidence about Romanesque military architecture.

A superlative fortress

Loarre, Aragon, eleventh – twelfth century, external view and plan. The outer wall is built of perfectly dressed oblong stones. The fortress proper comprises a court-yard (**1**), a chapel dedicated to the Virgin Mary (**2**), and a residential tower (**3**), the Tower of the Queen. In the late eleventh century a second curtain wall was built, with eight rounded towers open on the inside (**4**). The general plan of the fortress displays the careful siting of the buildings, with a typical double-curtain-wall plan in the less precipitous parts of the site.

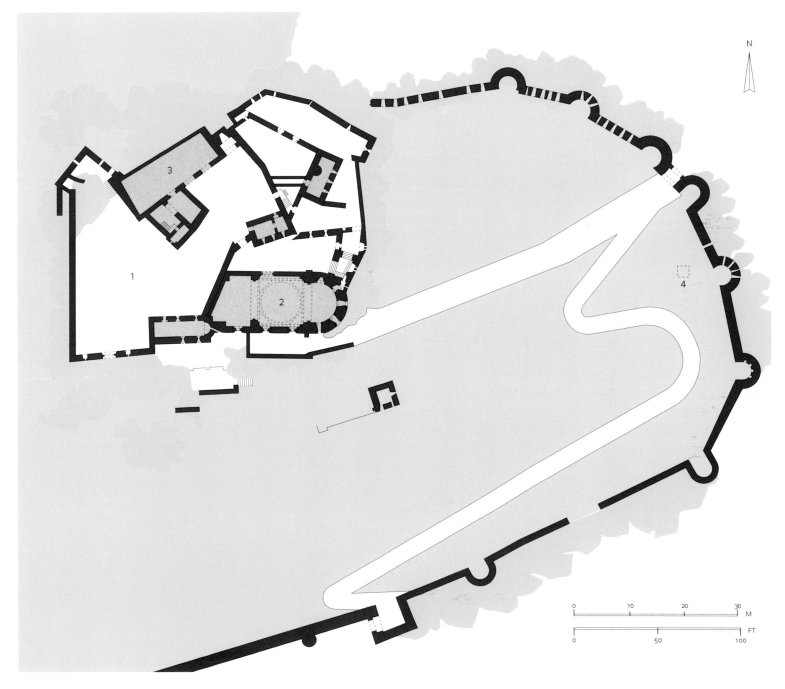

The city walls at Ávila are the masterpiece of twelfth-century Castilian fortifications. Constructed after the reconquest of the region from the Muslims, they are approximately rectangular in plan. There was no moat; the base is at ground level. The curtain wall, about 12 m high, is studded with semicircular towers; these are set some 20 m apart, and served not merely a defensive but a buttressing function. The town thus became a kind of collective fortress. The cathedral of Ávila was incorporated into the wall, its apse forming a separate machicolated tower. The houses of the nobles were built abutting the wall so that they could undertake their defensive duties in time of war.

A Castilian fortification
Covarrubias, curtain wall. The walls are studded with towers. The most famous of these is the Torre de Doña Urraca from the tenth century, which is 15 m long, 8 m wide and 18 m high. Its internal structure is analogous to those of French residential keeps.

The Village

A medieval village
Saint-Cirq-Lapopie, near Cahors. The steep site required that houses be built at successive levels. The density of the building around the parish church is clear; all the available space is used. Construction is not random: the largest houses are situated along the main street, while smaller houses are confined to the central zone, built along winding alleys so steep that they require stairs.

From the eleventh to the mid-thirteenth century, villages were founded at the initiative of a lord, or of two lords sharing the seigniory. Groups of peasants then settled in the centre of the land that they had to clear. One of the major characteristics of rural dwellings in the Middle Ages was their great mobility. This is particularly true of northern Europe; rural dwellings were more stable in the south. The centre of a village was its church and graveyard.

Excavation has helped us to establish three categories of medieval village. One comprised a main street on which individual properties were set at right angles, like the teeth of a comb, or obliquely, in herring-bone pattern. Other villages were on a grid plan, in which the layout of streets and properties is clear, indicating that equal amounts of land were allocated to each family in the village. Finally, some villages were on a central plan, but this was rare, and is particularly difficult to discern in the course of excavation. At a very early date we find villages in the south raised above the surrounding land. They generally consisted of a main road flanked by houses, with a chapel and a tower at opposite ends of the street. In the north we find large rural settlements

with hut foundations, silos, ditches and various other kinds of building.

General surveys and regional inventories have given us a fair knowledge of the castles and fortifications of the Middle Ages from the twelfth century on. But the subject of fortifications and fortified villages of the tenth century remains somewhat obscure. Villages attached to a castle generally had their own perimeter wall for defensive purposes, and this was also true of isolated villages. Such walls were of three kinds. The first was a curtain wall with towers. A second was formed by the continuously adjoining village houses, and lacked towers. A third, less well known, comprised one or more dry moats. In the case of smaller defensive walls, the parish church, itself sometimes fortified, formed the centre of the village.

The design of village houses was partly dictated by the lie of the land. They were built in mud or wood, and sometimes in rubblestone. They generally comprised a single room with a fire, poorly furnished and without decoration. Barns, cisterns and chapels, by contrast, were often built in regular courses. Vaulted, timber and tiled roofs were also found. The largest buildings

sometimes had several floors, and included doors and staircases, with windows for illumination. By the thirteenth century the use of stone meant that villages could no longer migrate as they had done in earlier times.

The domestic objects discovered in excavations are very diverse. In addition to fragments of pottery and tiles, there are many objects of iron: knives, nails, fastenings and tripods. Coins, glass and bone objects and stone grinding-wheels and mortars are also found. Naturally, the household objects of northern European villages differ in certain respects from those of the south.

Documents, sites, remains and the archaeological documentation of the period before the Middle Ages must all be studied in combination if we are to complete the picture afforded by archaeology and improve our understanding of the medieval fortified village. Knowledge of such villages is vital to our understanding of medieval demography, rural history and seigneurial incomes; lords who founded new villages did so in order to create new resources.

The Great Flowering of Romanesque

New Churches in France

Page 115

The art of the silversmith
Reliquary of the head of Saint Candidus, detail of the lower part. This scene is set within a square frame that forms the base of the bust of Saint Candidus, and shows the martyrdom of the Saint. The *repoussé* figures stand out in low relief from the flat background. This silver reliquary has survived in its original form, and is of prime importance for the study of medieval precious metalwork. (Treasury of the abbey of Saint-Maurice-d'Agaune)

A sample of the Church's treasures
Shrine of Saint Maurice, twelfth–thirteenth century, relief from the front side of the reliquary (57.5 cm high x 79.8 cm long x 35.7 cm wide). This is the Christ in Majesty, imparting the blessing with His right hand and holding a book in the other. At His feet are two of the symbols of the Evangelists: left, the eagle of Saint John; right, the winged man of Saint Matthew. The shrine is made of silver- and gold-plated copper plates adorned with cabochons. (Treasury of the abbey of Saint-Maurice-d'Agaune)

The South and the East

Two architectural tendencies predominated in twelfth-century Burgundy. The first of these is illustrated by the magnificent Cluny III. The foundations of the abbey church were laid in 1089; seven years later, Pope Urban II consecrated several of the abbey's altars while construction was still in progress. The building as a whole was consecrated in 1130. It was, alas, largely destroyed between 1798 and 1823. The south arm of the great transept has survived, along with the capitals of the apse. In addition to these vestiges, we know the building through old illustrations and through the archaeological research of Kenneth J. Conant.

Cluny III illustrated the economic vitality of the mother house of the Cluniac order; the plan of the church and adjacent buildings was determined by the requirements of the Order. The tall, graceful abbey church comprised a nave and four aisles, preceded by a narthex; there were two transepts, and an apse with ambulatory and radiating chapels. The façade was flanked by two towers.

Cluny III was the inspiration for many buildings in the region, including Saulieu, Autun, Semur-en-Brionnais and Langres. The priory church of Sainte-Croix-Notre-Dame at La Charité-sur-Loire is undoubtedly related to both Cluny II and Cluny III. The overall plan of Cluny III was repeated in the abbey church of Notre-Dame at Paray-le-Monial (begun before 1109), with certain modifications: a single transept, two aisles only, a three-storey elevation, and an ambulatory smaller in relation to the side-aisles than that of Cluny III. The same is true of Saint-Lazare at Autun, whose three-storey elevation is roofed with a pointed vault.

The main feature of the second tendency in Burgundian Romanesque is the use of groin vaulting in the nave. The most representative examples are those of Sainte-Madeleine at Vézelay, and the priory church of Sainte-Marie in Anzy-le-Duc. Construction of the nave of Sainte-Madeleine began in 1120. It is 10.2 m wide and 18.5 m high, groin-vaulted between semicircular transverse arches. The nave is preceded by a three-bay narthex of similar width, a type that was to play an important role in Burgundian Romanesque. The chevet stands above the crypt, and comprises five semicircular and four square chapels opening on to the ambulatory. Although the nave is one storey lower than that of Cluny III (there is no triforium), the direct lighting from the windows is not affected. In contrast with the Cluniac style, the emphasis at Vézelay is strongly horizontal.

In the Languedoc there are two distinct geographical areas: the southwest, including the Toulouse region, and the Mediterranean Languedoc (Provence). Artistic influences were transmitted between the southwest and the Poitevin and Saintonge areas further north via Périgord. The cathedrals of Bordeaux and of Petit-Palais in the Gironde are surviving examples of a design in which portals are flanked by two false bays resembling symbolic entrances to the side-aisles; columnar buttresses and rows of arcades reinforce the chevet.

The formula of chevet with ambulatory and radiating chapels spread from Burgundy to the Toulouse region and towards Quercy and the Albigeois; its influence is visible at Figeac and Gaillac. With it came the practice of roofing the nave with domes. Notable are the remains of the Romanesque cathedral at Albi, and, in Quercy, the tower-porch at Moissac. There the massive roof is reinforced by powerful diagonal ribs whose very low springing is supported by columns engaged in the walls of the square chamber.

The twelfth-century Romanesque of the Mediterranean Languedoc replaced rubblestone masonry with dressed stone carefully laid in courses. New buildings tended to adopt a single, very broad nave, with a continuous and sometimes pointed barrel vault. The persistence of the taste for a nave without side-aisles is exemplified by Saint-Pons, Agde, Saint-Papoul and Maguelone. Chevets sometimes took on quite complex forms, deriving from a range of styles; this is true of Saint-Jacques at Béziers and Saint-Nazaire at Carcassonne. We should also mention the fortified churches to be found throughout the Mediterranean area.

There are many local and regional variants of Romanesque. In the Auvergne, the example of the cathedral at Clermont-Ferrand influenced a whole series of buildings, notably Notre-Dame-du-Port and Saint-Saturnin in the same town, Saint-Paul at Issoire, Notre-Dame at Orcival, and Saint-Nectaire at Puy-de-Dôme. Most of these date from the first half of the twelfth century; they have a nave and side-aisles, a projecting transept with an apsidal chapel on each arm, a chevet with ambulatory and chapels radiating from the apse. Over the groin vaults of the aisles there are tribunes that buttress the central nave, on to which they open through double bays. A little indirect light reaches the nave from the tribune windows. The

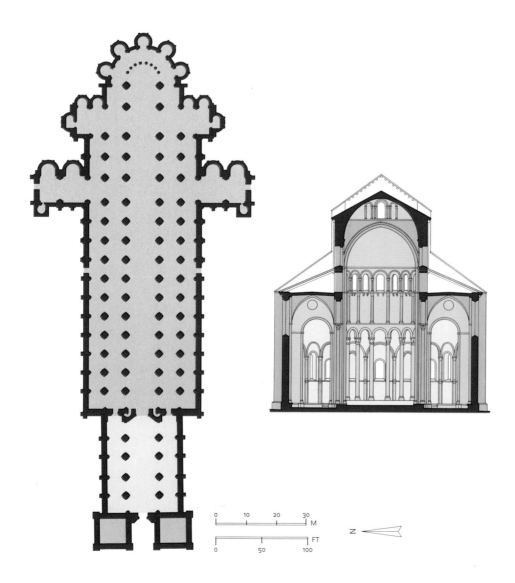

0 10 20 30
M
0 50 100
FT

Z

The most prestigious Romanesque abbey
Cluny III, 1089–1130, restored plan of the abbey church and cross-section of the choir. The plan of this remarkable building presented a nave and broad double aisles, east and west transepts, and a choir with ambulatory and five radiating chapels. The nave was preceded by a galilee with nave and aisles and a porch flanked by two towers. Its monumental proportions and the importance of the Cluniac order made this among the most influential buildings in the history of Romanesque architecture.

A smaller-scale version of Cluny
Notre-Dame, Paray-le-Monial, begun before 1109. The abbey church presents a single pair of transepts, but, like Cluny III, has an ambulatory smaller than the aisles and a three-level elevation. Here too we find a west narthex flanked by two towers. The model of Cluny inspired many churches, including those of Autun, Saulieu and Semur-en-Brionnais.

nave itself is roofed with a single barrel vault as far as the transept, where there is a dome on squinches. Volcanic stone and arkose (a type of sandstone) from the plain provide polychrome masonry, used to rhythmic effect in the chevets.

The abbey church of Notre-Dame-du-Port at Clermont-Ferrand (begun circa 1100) is regarded as the prototype of Auvergnat Romanesque. It has nave and side-aisles and a projecting transept with two apsidal east-facing chapels. The choir is composed of a single orthogonal bay and an ambulatory from which there radiate four semicircular apsidioles; there is no axial chapel. The nave has a continuous barrel vault without transverse arches, and is divided into five bays by alternating square and circular piers, each of which has three or four engaged colonnettes. The elevation is on two levels, with quadrant-vaulted tribunes. The wide windows of the groin-vaulted nave combine with the tribune openings to illuminate the nave

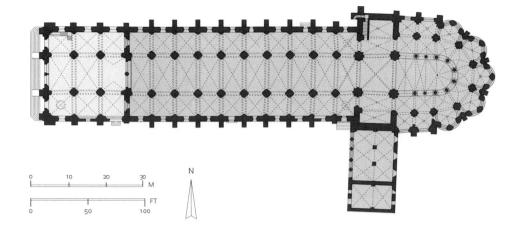

Simple architectural forms
Sainte-Madeleine, Vézelay, 1140–1150, plan. The three-bay narthex (1140– circa 1150) is the same width as the nave (1120– circa 1140) and aisles. The chevet is raised above the crypt, and comprises five circular and four square chapels opening on to the ambulatory. It was entirely rebuilt in Gothic style, circa 1185–1215.

The development of the façade
Sainte-Madeleine, Vézelay, west façade. The very large narthex with tribunes dates from the mid-twelfth century, and has a west façade comprising three portals and two towers. Forming a church in its own right, it was one of the last Burgundian narthexes to be built.

A semicircular composition

Sainte-Madeleine, Vézelay, tympanum of the south portal, circa 1125. On the lintel are depicted the Annunciation, Visitation and Nativity, on the tympanum the Adoration of the Magi. They complement the sculpted compositions of the north and central portals. An iconographic programme embracing several portals was exceptional in Romanesque art of the early twelfth century.

Theological synthesis

Sainte-Madeleine, Vézelay, central portal leading from narthex to nave, after 1120. The Mission of the Apostles, represented on the tympanum, was particularly significant during this, the period of the Crusades, when it was proclaimed that the duty of every Christian was to spread the Word. On the lintel are representatives of the pagan world, and on the archivolt the signs of the Zodiac are displayed alongside the Labours of the Months. The movements of the bodies and the treatment of the draperies confer great expressive intensity; we recognise here the influence of the Master of Cluny.

The didactic carver

Sainte-Madeleine, Vézelay, detail of a capital, after 1120. Between the bare astragal and the abacus decorated with foliated scrolls we see the figures of the Winds. With Old and New Testament scenes, the decoration formed part of a programme intended to aid the devotee to comprehend his faith.

A harmony of the vertical and the horizontal

Sainte-Madeleine, Vézelay, after 1120, nave. The nave is groin-vaulted with semicircular transverse ribs. The elevation is on two storeys. Voussoirs of alternating colours adorn the extrados of the transverse ribs and the arcades of the nave. Carved friezes of rosettes, ribbons and foliated scrolls emphasise the arcade, the string-courses of the windows, and the divisions of the elevation, articulating the architectural structure with great clarity.

Notre-Dame-du-Port, Clermont-Ferrand, circa 1100–1150, view from the south-west. The relatively narrow transept appears on the outside as an oblong massif towering over the roofs; beneath the polygonal bell-tower is the dome. The nave is divided into five bays, signalled on the outside by blind triplet bays in the upper part of the wall and blind arcades below. Chisel-curl brackets below the roof complete the ensemble.

Page 125

An enclosed interior
Notre-Dame-du-Port, Clermont-Ferrand, nave. The building material is arkose. Above the nave and crossing arcades, pebbles set in mortar create honeycomb effects. The nave has a semicircular barrel vault, and there are single aisles. The tribunes are quadrant-vaulted, with a semicircular transverse arch at every bay. They open on to the nave through trilobate cusped arches suggesting Arabic influence. Only the bay next to the crossing has semicircular arches.

indirectly. At the crossing, a dome on squinches is carried on four arcades; it is buttressed north and south by a narrow quadrant-vaulted bay, which matches the side-aisles. The projecting bay of the transept arms is roofed with a much lower barrel vault. The half-dome vault of the choir is much lower than that of the nave. The apse is particularly fine; on the capitals of its slender columns rest raised arches above which the windows lighting the choir are set in a further arcade. Externally, the combination of volumes is particularly happy; the effect of the buttresses is lightened by the carved cornices and modillions and the rich polychrome ornamentation of the walls.

Saint-Julien at Brioude is one of the most important pilgrimage sites in the whole of the Auvergne. It has a nave and aisles, a non-projecting transept, and an ambulatory at the chevet with radiating chapels. Le Puy is the site of a series of splendid

An audacious construction
Saint-Michel d'Aiguilhe, Le Puy, ambulatory. In the second half of the twelfth century, an ambulatory embracing the shape of the rock and surrounding a short nave was added to the pre-Romanesque building. The ambulatory is reached by five steps. This 'corridor' is bordered by a stone bench; the roof is formed of irregular groin vaults. The new building required the destruction of the porch and south apse of the original chapel.

Romanesque buildings: the cathedral, the baptistery of Saint-Jean, Saint-Michel-d'Aiguilhe, and the chapel of Saint-Clair. The cathedral at Le Puy is distinctive in that it does not share the plan used in the pilgrimage churches. It is now firmly established, as we noted above, that the presence in the cathedral of cusped arches and domes on squinches is not the sign of a putative Islamic influence. They were frequently used in the region, and from the twelfth century onwards form part of the ornamental repertory of both Mediterranean and Atlantic Romanesque.

A pre-Romanesque sanctuary
Saint-Michel d' Aiguilhe, Le Puy. The choir of the chapel is essentially the original building consecrated in 961. It rests directly on the rock, without foundations. It is an almost square room, which originally possessed three apses covered by a semi-dome vault. The central part of this building is surmounted by a pyramidal dome of four webs.

Ornamental and didactic friezes
Saint-Michel d'Aiguilhe, Le Puy, detail of the upper level of the façade, second half of the twelfth century. This part of the façade presents five niches each containing a bust. In the centre, Christ in Majesty, to the right the Virgin with halo and veil, proffering a vase, and to the left, the Archangel Michael. Below, the oculus is framed by four sets of palmettes on stalks.

Synthetic monumental iconography
Saint-Michel d'Aiguilhe, Le Puy, detail of the lower level of the façade, circa 1150–1165. The very simple portal displays two reclining sirens on its lintel. The first arch moulding is decorated with a tracery of foliage from which two heads emerge. Above this, a trefoil arcade represents the Adoration of the Lamb, with the Lamb at the centre surrounded by the symbols of the Evangelists and the Elders of the Apocalypse. This façade belongs to the final period of Romanesque sculpture in Le Puy.

Regional Schools and Their Exponents

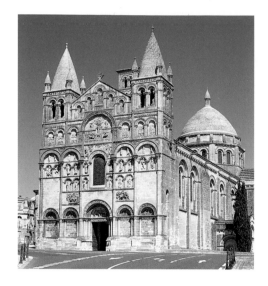

This history of medieval art does not depend exclusively on the history of events and on social and religious history. Two further sciences are at its service: geography and chronology. With their assistance, we can identify the birth of a style and the diffusion of influences, which together lead to the definition of regional style. As early as 1840, Arcisse de Caumont categorised Romanesque art in France into regional schools, basing his analysis on the external appearance of churches and on their ornamentation. He distinguished seven schools: northern France, with Champagne and the Orléanais; Normandy and Brittany; Poitou and the Angoumois; Aquitaine; Auvergne; Burgundy and Provence; and the provinces of the Rhineland. In the nineteenth century, the archaeologist Jules Quicherat based his theory of regional schools on the study of vaulting. The prevailing orthodoxy in monumental archaeology was at that time to treat buildings as though they were documents. Subsequently, Eugène Emanuel Viollet-le-Duc established his own system of regional schools, which included both Romanesque and Gothic churches.

During the first half of the twentieth century a number of nationalist schools arose, headed by strong personalities; one such was Josep Puig i Cadafalch, who attempted to define the origins of Romanesque. An architect and politician, he studied the monuments of Catalonia, northern Italy and the southern Adriatic in scrupulous detail in his quest to define the originality of these buildings both as series and as the expression of national groups. In France, other schools discussed the Romanesque regions and the question of which regional style preceded which. Notable practitioners include Eugène Lefèvre-Pontalis, Jean-Auguste Brutails, and Jean Vallery-Radot. Polemic concerning the chronology of regional style in France expanded to embrace national style: which came first, French or Spanish Romanesque? An eminent name here is that of Emile Mâle; American scholars such as Arthur Kingsley Porter also played a role in these debates.

In 1934 Henri Focillon's *La vie des formes* (The Life of Forms) quite transcended the regional debate by ascribing autonomous life to architectural forms. For Focillon, form is an essential of the work of art, and presides over its development. A brilliant medievalist, he turned his mind to the development of Romanesque in *Art des sculpteurs romans* (The Art of the Romanesque Sculptors), 1932, and to architecture in general in *Art d'Occident* (The Art of the West), which has been through many editions. In opposition to this formalist school was that of Pierre Francastel, who sought to integrate the work of art into the social, economic, geographical and regional context from which it arose, studying not just the work but the patron, the audience, the institution and the artist before turning to the work itself. This has been called the sociology of art.

Left

A frontispiece façade

Saint-Pierre, Angoulême, early twelfth century, west façade. The wall surface is animated by a network of five arcades in three registers, with smaller arcades in the upper part. The lantern towers and triangular gable are later additions.

Centre

The earliest Norman Romanesque

Notre-Dame, Bernay, completed in 1050. Originally a nave of seven bays opened on to narrow projecting transepts, each with single apsidiole. The two-bay choir was extended by a tripartite apse. Restoration in 1963 cleared and consolidated the nave. This is one of the earliest Romanesque buildings in Normandy.

Right

Ornament glorifying Christ

Saint-Pierre, Angoulême, detail of the ornament of the façade. Christ in Majesty is surrounded by a mandorla and the symbols of the four Evangelists. Angels are all about: above Christ, in the clouds and on the archivolt. The Romanesque ornamentation was restored in the nineteenth century.

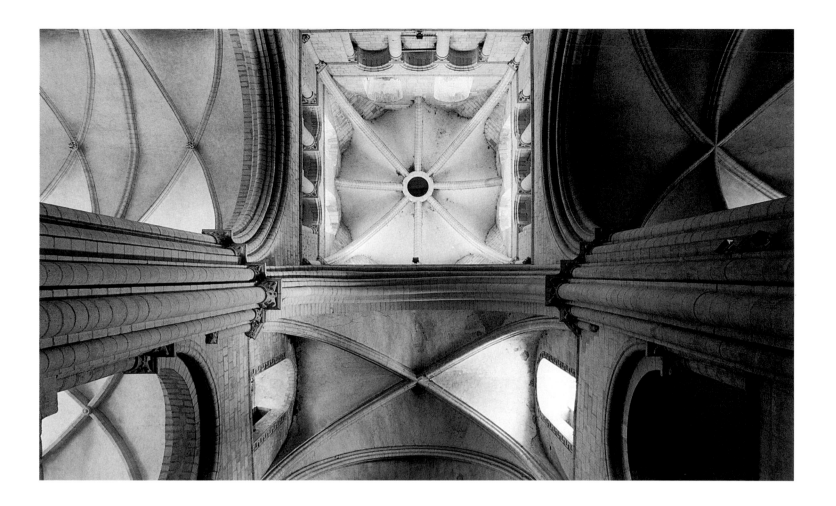

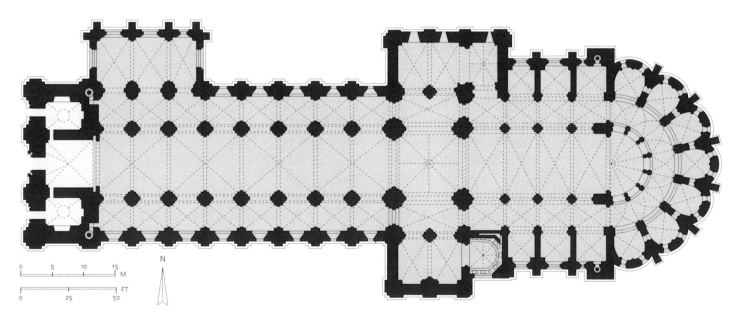

A clerestory lightens the walls
Saint-Étienne, Caen. The crossing originally carried an enormous lantern tower, which collapsed in 1566. The upper part here survives from that time, and contains two superposed passageways, the lower of which is completely blind.

Lower Normandy in the late eleventh century
Saint-Étienne, Caen, plan. The west façade comprises two powerful towers, whose verticality was enhanced by the addition of Gothic spires in the thirteenth century. The nave is divided into eight bays by piers with engaged columns. It leads into a projecting transept of two bays. The Gothic choir dates from the thirteenth century. Saint-Étienne testifies to the wave of monastic renewal that ran through Normandy at this period.

An airy and spacious interior
Saint-Étienne, Caen, nave wall, late eleventh century. The elevation is in three levels: arcade, tribunes of the same height as the arcade, and a clerestory in which the openings are divided by a column with capital. The tribune openings run the length of the side-aisles and round the transepts. They open on to the nave in arcades of the same size as the bays, without subdivision – a very rare arrangement in Norman Romanesque.

Page 131
An impressive chevet
Saint-Étienne, Caen, chevet. The choir was originally built on the Benedictine system with echelon chapels. Around 1200 it was replaced by a Gothic construction, comprising an ambulatory with seven radiating chapels, above which rise four slender pinnacles. This very original arrangement was imitated at Bayeux and Coutances.

Page 132

The abbey of the Seine Valley
Saint-Georges, Saint-Martin-de-Boscherville, chevet, early twelfth century. The choir consists of two orthogonal bays and a semicircular apse. There is a central tower at the crossing; each arm of the narrow transept has an apsidiole chapel.

Light floods the choir
Saint-Georges, Saint-Martin-de-Boscherville, interior of the apse. The internal elevation comprises two storeys. The lower level is lit by five bays with semicircular arches. The second level is more lively, with its five bays separated by short cylindrical piers.

A conventional façade
Saint-Georges, Saint-Martin-de-Boscherville. The central body of the façade is surmounted by a blind triangular gable that was raised during the Gothic period. On either side are two projecting towers. The central portal has a semicircular arch with bare tympanum.

The West and the North

In western France, Romanesque architecture can be classified by three large regions: Normandy, Brittany, and the areas of Poitou and Saintonge. The Romanesque of Normandy is of course closely related to that of England. Anglo-Norman art flourished from the third quarter of the eleventh century, with Caen as its centre. The principal characteristic of these buildings is a three-storey elevation with a clerestory and tribunes resting on large arcades. The façades are flanked by two symmetrical towers framing a gable. Though at first timber-roofed, they soon received rib vaults whose thick, heavy ribs are clumsily integrated into the nave wall on either side of the springing of the transverse arches. The depressed arches adopted by Anglo-Norman architects for rib vaulting required immensely thick walls that could absorb the thrust thus created.

A notable feature of buildings such as the abbey church of Saint-Georges at Saint-Martin-de-Boscherville, the priory church of Saint-Vigor at Cerisy-la-Forêt and the church of Saint-Étienne at Caen (the Abbaye-aux-Hommes) is a passage hollowed out of the thickness of the nave wall at clerestory level. This was also a feature of the earlier buildings at Bernay and Jumièges.

The Abbaye-aux-Dames (Sainte-Trinité) and the Abbaye-aux-Hommes (Saint-Étienne) at Caen exemplify the art of Lower Normandy in the late eleventh century. Both have a nave and side-aisles with projecting transept and an elongated chevet. Sainte-Trinité, founded between 1059 and 1065, has, in its apse, a perfect example of the thick wall characteristic of Norman architecture; the wall is effectively double. The Abbaye-aux-Hommes, which dates from about 1063, is distinctive in its possession of tribune galleries above the side-aisles; they are pierced with windows that occupy the entire width of the bays without any subdivision. Here too there is a gallery at clerestory level, which opens on to the nave in the form of a high portico. The west end is divided into three unequal parts by the four buttresses; it has two registers of small windows with semicircular arches, above which stand the two massive towers with their ornamentation of blind arcades.

One of the finest achievements of Romanesque art in the early twelfth century is the abbey church of Saint-Georges at Saint-Martin-de-Boscherville in Upper Normandy. It is a large building; the nave is 15.8 m high and around 8.6 m wide. It follows the tradition of the major Norman churches built in the period of William the

Conqueror: chevet with echelon chapels, apse lit by two rows of windows, lantern tower at the crossing, and a long nave divided into bays by arcades resting on piers flanked by columns and colonnettes. Its three-storey elevation, luminous interior and play of architectural volumes constitute an outstanding success. A single support carries the tribune galleries that run around the arms of the transept, presenting narrow openings just below the roof, which are incorporated into the series of ornamental blind arcades. They are typical of the architecture of this period, and, like the architectural decoration of the apse, have their equivalents in Saint-Nicholas in Caen.

Other autonomous forms of Romanesque architecture are found around Poitiers and towards the Saintonge region. These are wide buildings, with aisles as high as the nave. The nave is covered with a semicircular barrel vault on transverse arches

Page 135

Sumptuous ornament
Notre-Dame-la-Grande, Poitiers, first half of the twelfth century, façade. The angle buttresses of clustered columns rise to conical roofs decorated with scales. In the centre, a deep portal with four rows of archivolts is framed by two sets of slightly pointed blind arcades. The whole surface of the façade is animated with blind arcades and extensive sculpted decoration, and perfectly exemplifies the Romanesque façades of Poitou and Saintonge.

Simple figurative decoration
Saint-Georges, Saint-Martin-de-Boscherville, early twelfth century, relief from the tribune of the north transept. A king or bishop sits on a throne holding a cross in his left hand, and blesses with the other. The stone was cut out around the feet, which rest on two human heads.

Harmonious architecture
Saint-Georges, Saint-Martin-de-Boscherville, interior. The nave is divided into eight bays by cruciform piers with engaged half-columns. The tritorium bays each contain four tall, narrow arcades on colonnettes set into square pilasters. The clerestory has large bays with semicircular arches; a narrow passage is cut into the wall.

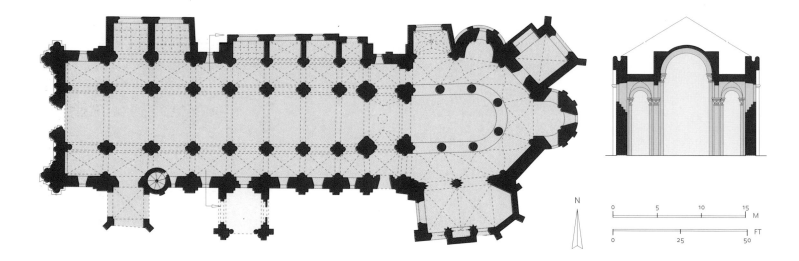

(Notre-Dame-la-Grande in Poitiers, Saint-Savin-sur-Gartempe) or a pointed barrel vault on transverse arches (Saint-Pierre, Aulnay). The tower is at the crossing. The roofs of the bell-towers are often cone-shaped, with ornamental fish-scale patterns in the stone tiling. The façade of Notre-Dame-la-Grande in Poitiers (completed circa 1150) is typical of this group; rich carved ornament covers the entire surface. The portal is flanked by slightly smaller blind bays and surmounted by two registers of small blind arcades interrupted only by the great axial window. The abbey church of Saint-Sauveur in Charroux has an extraordinary layout that combines elements of basilican and central plans: a porch bell-tower leads into the nave, which is completed by a triple rotunda with a triple ambulatory lit by a central lantern tower. Beneath the rotunda is a crypt. Finally, the church of Saint-Savin-sur-Gartempe (1060–1115) is remarkable both for its innovative architecture and its fine murals.

Brittany's geographical position facilitated artistic dialogue with England, Anjou, Poitou and La Vendée, and subsequently with Normandy. The remarkable central-plan churches of Sainte-Croix in Quimperlé and Lanleff somewhat resemble the rotunda of Neuvy-Saint-Sépulcre in Berry. The abbey churches of Saint-Gildas-de-Rhuys and Landévennec (late eleventh to early twelfth centuries) show a plan not often found in Brittany: nave and side-aisles, extended choir with ambulatory and radiating chapels. More common is a basilican plan with one or three rectangular or semicircular apses. The nave and aisles are generally low, and the single-storey elevation allows direct lighting of the nave. The roof is generally of timber. Schist, granite and sometimes sandstone are put to excellent use in the architectural ornament.

In the Champagne region, the North and the Île-de-France the transition to Gothic took place unusually early. The architectural traditions of the first millennium survived the eleventh century and part of the twelfth. Churches in the Champagne region are light in structure and have timber roofs. In the Marne, the timber-roofed nave of the church at Courville offers a good example of this style. The priory of Saint-Martin-des-Champs, a daughter house of Cluny, was founded in Paris by Henri I in 1060 and consecrated seven years later. It has a choir with a wide ambulatory approximately contemporary with that of Saint-Denis. Today, it houses a museum. In the period 1120–1140 small buildings in the Île-de-France were often the focus of experiment with architectural innovations, such as the intersecting rib vault. These initiatives proliferated with the development of the Gothic.

The Romanesque of western France

Notre-Dame-la-Grande, Poitiers, first half of the twelfth century, plan and cross-section. The very long nave of nine bays is flanked by narrow side-aisles, and opens directly on to the choir, ambulatory and radiating chapels; there is no transept. The crossing is signalled by massive piers supporting a dome. The very high groin vaults of the aisles have the effect of making nave and aisles into a single space.

Ornamental exuberance

Notre-Dame-la-Grande, Poitiers, first half of the twelfth century, detail of the façade. The tripartite division of the façade is underlined by broad horizontal cornices. On the first level the sculpted figures are placed in the spandrels of the blind arcade, forming a single composition across the face of the façade. The scenes are from the Old and New Testaments. Under the two levels of blind arcades of the upper register are sculpted apostles and two holy bishops.

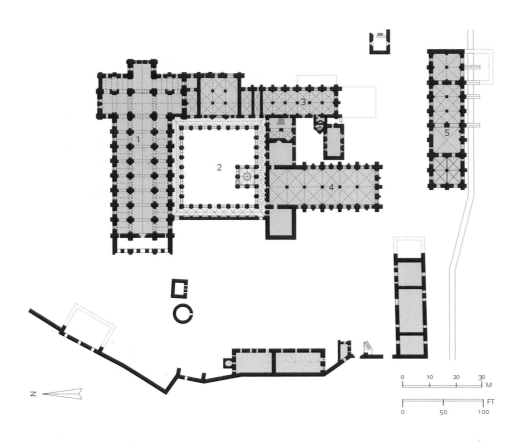

The model for Cistercian abbeys
Fontenay, completed 1147, plan of the monastery. A wall encloses the church and monastic buildings. In the centre, the cloister adjoins the church, which stands opposite the refectory. The church is in Latin-cross plan; nave and aisles lead to huge transepts; the two flat-backed chapels were originally walled off from the transept. The rectangular apse stands in for a choir. The austerity of Cistercian architecture is similarly reflected in the monastic buildings: chapterhouse, sacristy and calefactory.
1 Church
2 Cloister
3 Refectory
4 Great hall
5 Work building

Cluniac and Cistercian Buildings

Around the first millennium, the arts were strongly influenced by the resurgence in Western monasticism. From the early ninth century to the early twelfth century the Benedictine movement was at its height. It was born in the rule established at Monte Cassino shortly after 534 by Saint Benedict of Nursia. The first attempts at reformation took place during the first half of the tenth century, thanks to the efforts of such energetic men as Mayeul and Odilo. These two men went from monastery to monastery preaching purity and respect for the Benedictine rule. The most important centre of reform at this period was the Burgundian abbey of Cluny, founded in 910 by Guillaume the Pious of Aquitaine. Cluny rapidly established a wide network of dependent monasteries, and thus encouraged the diffusion of Romanesque architecture.

The prestige of the order is exemplified by the monumental character of Cluny II and Cluny III. The plan of Cluny III comprised a double transept, a choir with radiating chapels and exceptionally lofty vaulting. The influence of these buildings is clear in many Burgundian churches, such as Saint-Lazare at Autun and the abbey church of Notre-Dame at Paray-le-Monial, as we have seen; they give some idea of the scale of Cluny III. The churches of Sainte-Madeleine at Vézelay and Saint-Lazare at Autun similarly give some notion of the style of the choir of Cluny III and of the quality of its carved capitals. The small priory of Berzé-la-Ville, in its turn, offers some idea of the painted decoration of the abbey at Cluny.

The Cistercian order was created in Burgundy by Robert de Molesme, who founded Cîteaux in 1098. It was a reaction against the life at Cluny, which assigned somewhat less importance to an ascetic lifestyle. The Cistercian rule, with its requirements of poverty, work and silence, originated a new kind of church architecture, which combined extreme austerity with a remarkable purity of line enhanced by very high standards of masonry. This form of architecture began to develop widely under the impulse of Saint Bernard, who was a monk of Clairvaux after 1115. Fontenay abbey, built between 1139 and 1140, is typical of Cistercian

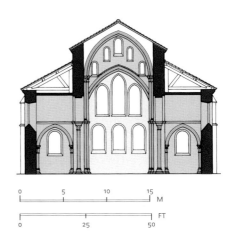

The Cistercian chevet
Fontenay, cross-section of the church, 1139–1147. The east and west ends are pierced with sets of three windows in order to light the nave. Most Cistercian churches adopted rectangular flat-ended chevets. Since the Cistercian liturgy was conducted in the nave, there was no need for an enlarged east end.

Simple, spiritual forms
Fontenay, completed 1147, cloister. The cloister, too, exhibits the Cistercian principles of simplicity and austerity. There monks would meditate, pray, read and labour. The purity of form and absence of ornament are wholly at one with the spiritual aspirations of the Cistercian order.

Bare walls in the abbey church
Fontenay, north aisle of the abbey church, 1139–1147. The elevation of the nave is particularly austere; there is no clerestory. Light enters indirectly, through the windows of the aisles. The nave has a pointed barrel vault with transverse ribs, and is buttressed by the transverse barrel vaults of the aisles. This architectural formula was repeated by the Cistercians throughout Europe.

Cistercian rectitude

Fontenay, completed 1147. The galleries are roofed with a pointed barrel vault, whose thrust is absorbed by the massive buttresses. The semicircular arcades open on to the garth. Relieving arches span the paired arches resting on short, paired colonnettes.

Severe ornament

Fontenay, completed 1147, detail of a cloister capital. The capitals display a repertory of flat leaf motifs whose elegantly curved tips soften the angles. These carvings contrast with the strictly geometrical necks of the capitals in the abbey church. The austerity of the church is thus relaxed somewhat in the cloister, a place for transit and restorative meditation.

architecture. Its great simplicity is a reflection of Cistercian ideals; it has a cruciform plan and great simplicity in the elevation of nave and side-aisles. The capitals are sometimes carved, but only with geometric motifs.

The innovative architecture of Fontenay finds expression in very severe lines; they were the proper expression of the order's anti-Cluniac spirit. The church has nave and side-aisles, a projecting transept and flat chevet; the pointed barrel vault is carried on transverse arches. The nave is lit directly through large windows in the triumphal arch and the façade and indirectly through the windows of the side-aisles. This type of building is directly comparable to Burgundian Romanesque. Cistercian architecture played an important part in the introduction of the Gothic style not only in France, but in Spain and Catalonia.

Cistercian cloisters also have a beautiful austerity at one with the activities that they accommodated: meditation, prayer and manual labour. The *scriptoria* of Cistercian monasteries similarly observed a severity contrasting with the luxury of manuscripts copied by other orders. The early use of intersecting rib vaults, which spread with the Cistercian order, was one of the keys to the transition between Romanesque and Gothic, as can be seen at Pontigny.

The abbey of Sénanque in the Vaucluse is a fine example of a southern Cistercian complex. Founded in 1148 under the protection of its mother institution in Simiane, the abbey flourished after the arrival of monks from Mazan. Construction of the church began barely ten years after the foundation of the house, and lasted for some forty years. Unusually, the church is oriented to the north. Its plan is similar to that of Le Thoronet: a nave and side-aisles, a wide transept and five apses. The latter part of the building seems likely to be the oldest; it is, in any case, highly original, with a projecting semicircular apse flanked on either side by two apsidioles. The apsidioles are also semicircular, but integrated with the north wall of the transept. The nave is somewhat later, and roofed with a pointed tunnel vault entirely lacking in transverse arches.

An example of a provincial abbey Sénanque, late twelfth century, general view. The abbey church is not oriented east–west; its chevet faces north. The standard monastic buildings, to the left of the church, are therefore west of it. Conventionally they would be sited to the north. The confined site and the limit set to the extent of the monks' and lay brothers' building by the stream flowing north to south forced the monks to break a rule very widely observed in the Middle Ages.

As prescribed by Saint Bernard
Sénanque, late twelfth century, detail of a capital from the cloister. The twin columns of the cloister galleries display various forms of decoration on their capitals. There are leaves and flowers whose upper edges form volutes beneath the abacus, cable moulding, palmettes, and tracery decorated with pearls. The exquisitely carved ornament adds to the beauty of the cloister.

A cloister for spiritual restoration
Sénanque, cloister. On a square plan, with large square pillars at each corner, the cloister presents a semicircular barrel vault with square-section transverse ribs. The galleries give on to the garth via twelve semicircular arcades resting on pillars alternating with two pairs of twin colonnettes. The latter share their base and abacus.

Page 145

**The full maturity of the
Cistercian style**

Silvacane, 1175–1230, interior of
the abbey church. The nave and
side aisles extend into the vast
transept, which has two flat-
ended chapels in each arm. The
chevet is of the same width as the
nave; the flat end wall is pierced
with three bays with semicircular
arches and an eight-lobed oculus.

The transverse ribs of the vaults
rest on engaged columns set into
pilasters. The harmony of the
proportions, the beauty of the
masonry, and the elegance of
the very sober capitals testify
to the full maturity attained by
Cistercian architecture.

Pure lines

Silvacane, façade. It is divided
into three sections by powerful
buttresses. The central portal has
double semicircular archivolts
resting on capitals decorated
with leaves folded into crockets.
Above the door are three narrow
windows surmounted by an
oculus. The triangular gable
and the lateral pent roofs are
underlined with modillions. The
sobriety of the composition is
at one with Cistercian ideals.

Cistercian expansion in Switzerland
Notre-Dame, Bonmont-sur-Nyon
1131 – mid-twelfth century.
The priory of Bonmont was
built north-west of Nyon by
Benedictines of the *comtois*
convent of Balerne in 1120, before
Burcard introduced the Cistercian
rule there in 1136. This priory
church is one of the oldest Cistercian buildings in west Switzerland.

A simple portal for a Cistercian priory
Notre-Dame, Bonmont-sur-Nyon,
west portal. The west façade
possesses a portal with moulded
archivolts; the slightly pointed
arch rests on the columns in the
splay of the door. The sculpted
motifs of the capitals are almost
the only form of ornament.

The cloister and dependent buildings belong to the turn of the century and stand to the east of the church. The rich ornamental detailing of this cloister has often been remarked on, and, as at Fontenay and Escale-Dieu, it contrasts noticeably with the austerity of the basilica. The capitals are sculpted with leaves, flowers, cable moulding, palmettes and interlace. Chapter house, dormitory, refectory, calefactory and lay brethren's quarters complete one of the most evocative of Cistercian monastic complexes.

The abbey of Le Thoronet is effectively contemporary with Sénanque; it was founded in 1136 by monks from Mazan. The masonry of the abbey church is beautifully organised rubblestone of medium size. It too was begun around 1160, but the process of construction was much more rapid than at Sénanque; Le Thoronet was completed in twenty-five years. The plans of the two abbeys, and more particularly of their chevets, are almost identical. Both are typical of the earlier Cistercian churches. A wide nave is flanked by low side aisles and divided into three bays. It leads to a projecting transept, which has four lateral apsidioles in the thickness of its walls. Like the projecting central apse, these are semicircular and preceded by a vertical bay. Pointed barrel vaults predominate, except in the side-aisles, where a

An austere Cistercian interior
Notre-Dame, Bonmont-sur-Nyon, 1131 – mid-twelfth century. The church has lost its original chevet, which followed the Cistercian format of a flat chevet leading from low transepts. The nave is covered with a semicircular barrel vault. The simplicity of this interior, entirely lacking in ornament, faithfully respects Cistercian tradition.

The fountain: a functional element in the cloister
Cistercian abbey, Poblet, cloister fountain, circa 1200. The fountain is set under a hexagonal kiosk with a ribbed vault. It was intended principally for the ablutions of the monks. Besides the practical purpose, the fountain was a symbol of the Fountain of Life.

quadrant vault on transverse arches buttresses the pointed barrel vault of the nave. A door in the north arm of the transept led to the sacristy, and from there a staircase led up to the dormitory. The monastic buildings are to the north, set around a cloister that seems to derive from that of Silvacane.

The cloister at Le Thoronet is famous for its austere appearance and lack of architectural ornament. It is on an elongated trapezoidal plan, and the arcades are grouped into pairs separated by a sturdy column with a plain capital. In the garth, at the middle of the north gallery, is the lavabo pavilion, a piece of architecture fundamental to the daily rhythm of monastic life. As at Sénanque and Silvacane, the dormitory is an exemplary piece of utilitarian religious architecture. It is a huge room roofed with a pointed barrel vault on transverse arches, 8 m high at its highest point, and lit on two sides by narrow windows with semicircular arches.

Above left

The floral capital

Le Thoronet, circa 1160–1200, detail of a capital. The arches rest directly on the capital without an intervening abacus. The capital is adorned with the tightly compressed curves of high-relief volutes. This very sober ornament is perfectly suited to the simplicity of the architecture.

Above right

Compact architectural forms

Le Thoronet, detail of the cloister galleries. The choice of a stone roof for the galleries made particularly sturdy supports necessary. The squat arcades have their semicircular arches divided by a heavy and slightly convex central column, crowned by a sculpted capital and with an oculus.

The cloister garth as garden

Le Thoronet, cloister. The cloister has four vaulted galleries. The south gallery has a semicircular barrel vault, which in the later galleries has become sharply pointed. The monastic buildings are arranged around the cloister according to Cistercian tradition. To the south of the church are the sacristy and chapterhouse. The purity of line and perfection of the masonry of Cistercian buildings impart a beauty that transcends their austerity.

The Symbolism of Romanesque Buildings

The work of Gislebertus
Saint-Lazare, Autun, tympanum of the west portal, circa 1130. The Last Judgment is represented with Christ in Majesty at the centre and on either side the damned and the saved. The elongated bodies, billowing drapery and emphasis on parallels are some of the aspects of Gislebertus's originality. The artist signed his name at the feet of the Christ: 'Gislebertus hoc fecit' – Gislebertus has made this.

Among the many authors who wrote during the Romanesque period about the symbolism of the religious building, Honorius of Autun, who lived in the first half of the twelfth century, is among the most profound. Today he is a little-known author, whose period of popularity between 1095 and 1135 was partly due to his *De gemma animae* (Jewel of the Soul) consisting of four books. In this work, especially in the first book, Honorius follows in the footsteps of the Church Fathers and draws on New Testament passages to consider the Christian temple as a prefiguration of the New Jerusalem. Like other medieval writers, he seeks in the New Testament a symbolic significance for each element of a church.

Architecture, as a part of the universe, is a lasting manifestation of the divine project. The artisan who builds it and the Christians who enter it can perceive in the fabric of the building an analogue of the harmony of a world governed by God and of the eternal life that awaits them.

In the late twelfth and very early thirteenth centuries, Sicardus, Bishop of Cremona and a great liturgist (circa 1155–1215), composed his work *Mitrale* or Churchbook drawing on Honorius's theories. In it, he widened and deepened the quest for a mystical and theological symbolism attached to each element of temple and monastery. Later, in the second half of the thirteenth century, the Bishop of Mande, Guilelmus Durandus the Elder (circa 1230–1296), wrote his *Rationale divinorum officiorum* or Manual of Services, which is the most complete treatise on the function and symbolism of churches and on liturgical rites.

According to Honorius of Autun, the temple or church is the symbol in this world of the temple of glory in the New Jerusalem. In the celestial Temple, the Church celebrates the divinity in constant peace. It is divided in two, for the temple of the heavenly court discriminates between angels and men.

Churches are oriented towards the east, whence the sun rises, because the 'sun of justice' is venerated in the east, and in the east, too, is paradise, our home according to Honorius. The material church symbolises the Church: that is, the community of the faithful gathered for divine service. The material church rests on stone foundations, just as the Church rests on the rock of Christ. It rises towards heaven in the form of its four walls, while the Church grows through the virtues of the Four Gospels. The house of prayer built in solid stone symbolises the strength created by the faith and works of the Church. Stones bonded by mortar are the faithful bonded by love. The sanctuary symbolises the primitive Church, born of the Jews, while the nave represents those who serve God in active life.

The transparent windows, which exclude the storm but allow in the light, are doctors who fight heresies and spread the light of the Church's teachings. The glass of the windows through which the rays of light pass are the thoughts of the doctors, who perceive divine matters as if through a glass.

The columns that support the house of God symbolise the bishops, on whom the structure of the Church rests, thanks to their upright lives. The beams that ensure the stability of the building are the powerful of this world who offer their protection to the Church. The tiles of the roof, which prevent rain entering the building, are the soldiers who protect the Church against pagans and enemies.

The paintings decorating the ceiling and the walls provide examples for the just, and represent the customary decoration of the Church. The paintings are executed for three reasons: first, to be read by the lay person; second, to decorate the building; and third, to commemorate our predecessors in life.

The pavement underfoot is the people thanks to whose work the Church is sustained. The crypts, constructed beneath ground level, are those who cultivate the inner life. The altar on which the sacrifice is offered is Christ, thanks to Whom the sacrifice of the Church is accepted. The Body of Christ is so clearly manifest on the altar that the people believe in Him; thus they can, thanks to Him, be born again and united with Him, just as the individual stones of which it is made are united to constitute the altar.

Relics are hidden within the altar because all the treasures of wisdom and knowledge are contained in Christ. On the altar are placed reliquaries of the apostles and martyrs who suffered for Christ. The altar cloths are confessors and virgins, whose actions are the ornament of Christ.

The cross stands on the altar for three reasons: first, because it is the sign of our King in the House of God, that is, in the Royal City, to be adored by the soldiers; second, in order to represent the Passion constantly; and finally, so that Christians imitate Christ and crucify in their own flesh their own passions and desires.

The ciborium holding the Eucharist and placed on the altar is the divinity of Christ, offered as a sacrifice for the human race. The steps by which one reaches the altar are the virtues by which we attain to Christ. The lavabo near the altar used for the ritual washing of the celebrant's hands is the mercy that proceeds from Christ and through which humankind is liberated from its burden of sin through baptism and penitence.

The cloths hung in the church are the miracles of Christ, and the ambo, from which the lesson is read, represents the lives of the just. The church is constantly lit by lamps just as the Church of Christ is eternally illuminated by the flame of the Holy Spirit.

The chandelier made from different kinds of metal symbolises good works: gold for martyrs, silver for virgins, copper for those who curb their passions, and iron for those who submit to their spouses. Precious stones symbolise those who are remarkable for their virtues.

The door of the building is intended to obstruct the passage of enemies and to open the way for friends; it is thus Christ, who expels the infidel from the House of God and opens himself to the faithful.

The towers are the two laws by which the preachers (bells) announce the divine kingdom, as if they were suspended from the celestial heights over terrestrial things. The sound of the bells represents preaching. The rope that rises to the height of the tower is a prayer eloquent of celestial themes. The weathercock set on the summit of the bell-tower awakens those who sleep, as does the priest. The cemetery, the dormitory of the dead, is the bosom of the Church.

The cloister stands close to the monastic church, as the porch of Solomon stood close to the Temple. It prefigures Paradise; the monastery is thus the Garden of Eden, the securest part of Paradise. In Eden is the fountain of life; in the monastery are the baptismal fonts. In Paradise is the Tree of Life, just as in the monastery we find the Body of the Lord. The monastery presages Paradise, with its closed cloister in the image of heaven, where the just are separated from the sinners just as those who profess the religious life are kept apart from secular existence.

As regards the form of the church, Honorius of Autun is very explicit. Cruciform churches testify to the way in which the people of the Church must be crucified for the world. Circular-plan churches show that the Church, through love, stands on the entire perimeter of the Orb, like a crown of eternity.

Honorius of Autun and his twelfth-century followers built a theological and mystical structure that clothed the religious building in symbolism, showing that its every component part precisely figured an aspect of the divine order.

Cathedrals and Monasteries

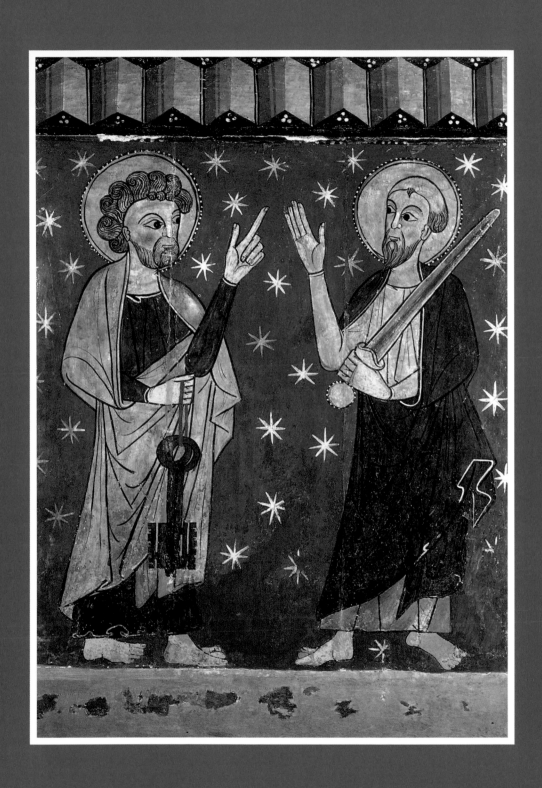

A Tide of New Building
in Southern Europe

Page 153
Emotions expressed in stone
This carved relief from Modena cathedral shows Adam and Eve covering their nakedness with leaves. Their bodies are short and sturdy. Their faces are full of anxiety concerning their sin, to which the menacing finger clearly alludes. This detail perfectly summarises the expressiveness of Romanesque sculpture.

Church furniture in painted wood
Lateral part of a Catalan altar, tempera on wood. To the left we see Saint Peter with the keys, to the right Saint Paul holding the instrument of his martyrdom, the sword, which is often identified with the sword of Judgment. This late Romanesque painting, with its intense colours, exemplifies the admirable qualities of Catalan Romanesque altar frontals. (Museu Arqueologic-Artistic Episcopal, Vic)

The Iberian Peninsula

Romanesque architecture flourished in Spain over a period of some two hundred years, from the early eleventh to the late twelfth century. Its territory was constantly expanding as the Spanish reconquest progressed. Three great periods can be identified: the first, the mature and the late Romanesque, the latter of which overlaps with early Gothic.

In the twelfth century, the northern states of the Iberian peninsula, and in particular the *condado* of Barcelona, displayed a spirit of fierce independence towards both Saracens and Franks, and indeed towards each other. Many campaigns against the Islamic occupation resulted. The Romanesque style followed a pattern of local development influenced by political and social conditions, technical progress and wealthy local patrons who issued commissions and encouraged artistic exchanges with other parts of the world. This Romanesque first emerged in regions where political authority and military frontiers were firmly established.

The earliest Romanesque architecture began to appear in the kingdom of Navarre and the *condado* of Barcelona in the first quarter of the twelfth century. Josep Puig i Cadafalch initially identified the first southern Romanesque, pointing out features shared by Catalan, southern French and northern Italian buildings: blind arcading, pilaster strips, a style of masonry that used small stones, and stone vaulting. Henri Focillon noted that it was the southern equivalent of the Ottonian art of northern and Germanic Europe. Romanesque architecture spread rapidly through Catalonia during the first three-quarters of the eleventh century, under the impulse of two factors. The first was the multiple contacts with the outside world initiated under abbots such as Guarin and Oliba. The second was the various pilgrimages, which brought artistic influences into Catalonia in their wake. Thanks to these contacts, the first Romanesque buildings in Catalonia were built by Lombard master-masons. They were normally basilican in plan, with nave and side-aisles and a transept separating the nave from the chevet.

This was a multi-faceted style. Thus at the abbey church of Saint-Michel-de-Cuxa (France), which was enlarged at Abbot Oliba's behest early in the eleventh century, two monumental towers were built on the arms of the transept, and a false ambulatory with apsidioles constructed around the chevet. The basilica of Ripoll has four side-aisles and a transept with no less than seven aligned apses, somewhat like those of Old Saint Peter's in Rome. We should also mention the abbey church of Sant Pere de Rodes (San Pedro de Roda), whose superposed orders and chevet with ambulatory were inspired by classical canons and Lombard proportions; the collegiate church of Sant Vicenç (San Vicente) at Cardona, with its carefully composed volumes; and the collegiate church of Sant Pere (San Pedro) at Ager. There are few traces of the great early Romanesque cathedrals, such as those of Barcelona, Vic and Gerona; they were mostly replaced by Gothic or neo-classical constructions. It is thus impossible to reconstitute these ensembles in the mind's eye; in many cases, only archaeological evidence and vestigial ruins have survived.

A renowned Cistercian abbey
Poblet, general view. The abbey was founded in the mid-twelfth century by Cistercian monks from Fontfroide, on land donated by Count Ramón Berenguer IV. It presents all the characteristics of the Cistercian monastery: within the enclosure wall are church, cloister, chapterhouse, dormitory, refectory and a royal palace, in addition to the library, cellar and other outbuildings. Its size and architectural quality (there has been little alteration) give the complex at Poblet an important place in the history of Cistercian architecture.

In the kingdoms of western Spain the first traces of the Romanesque date from the quest for political unification undertaken by Sancho III the Great of Navarre (1000–1035). Sancho, no traditionalist, was closely linked to the Catalan prelates; in consequence, the earliest Romanesque buildings of Navarre closely resemble the major Catalan monuments. This was a time of large-scale projects. Construction of the cathedral of Pamplona began, San Juan de la Peña was enlarged, and the abbey of San Salvador at Leyre was reconstructed; the monastery at Leyre is considered the major work of this early Romanesque. The monastery is built in courses of large stones, and possesses an enormous crypt.

Fernando I of Castile (1035–1065) extended his kingdom by conquest, taking over territories that left their mark on the art produced under his patronage. The new form of capital introduced in the nave and porch of San Pedro at Teverga was effectively Visigothic in style. During the reign of Alfonso VI of Castile (1072–1109) various events favoured the diffusion of Romanesque: in 1080, the Roman liturgy was adopted; marriages created links between Castile, León, Aragon and Navarre. And the reconquest of Spain now took on the air of a Crusade. The Santiago de Compostela pilgrimage route was reorganised to cope with the vast influx of pilgrims. Taken together, these circumstances limited French influence in the creation of Spanish Romanesque.

The first fully mature Romanesque buildings appeared on the Santiago pilgrimage route in the last quarter of the eleventh century. The cathedrals and churches along the route reveal a tendency towards an architecturally unified style arising from the need to accommodate large processions. The Romanesque style spread through most of Spain in the wake of the reconquest.

Two forms of Romanesque architecture predominated in the twelfth century. The first of these, deriving from the first southern Romanesque, was limited, for the most part, to Catalonia. The second, a more mature style, arose in the recently reconquered Navarro-Aragonese and Castilian-Aragonese territories. French innovations slowly made their influence felt. Donations to the Cistercians were increasingly frequent during the reigns of Alfonso VII (1126–1157) and the Conde de Barcelona, Ramón Berenguer IV (1131–1162). Elements of the Gothic style, such as the ribbed vault and pointed arch, were introduced in the cathedrals of Tarragona, Lleida (Lérida), Zamora and Salamanca.

Second Romanesque

Sant Pere de Galligans, Gerona, twelfth century. The nave and aisles extend into the transept and a round apse. On one side of the apse are two apsidioles; on the other is a larger apsidiole chapel, which is combined with an apsidal chapel grafted on to the end of the transept arm. This odd layout suggests that an earlier church with three apsidal chapels in a semicircle was incorporated into the Romanesque construction. An octagonal two-storeyed lantern tower dominates the building.

Catalan Romanesque

Cathedral of Santa Maria, La Seu d'Urgell, before 1131–1180, chevet. There are two apsidioles hollowed out of the wall on either side of the very long transept. Only the central part of the apse projects from the chevet; it contains a gallery that extends round into the transepts. From the outside it shows as a series of arcades resting on twin granite columns with capitals. This arrangement is found in many north Italian churches.

Page 159 above left
The cathedral in the city

Santa Maria, façade. The body of the building is framed by massive buttresses. Above the archivolts of the central door are three windows; above this a triangular gable with a chevron frieze has one central window and two oculi. Over the façade rises a square bell-tower.

Page 159 below left
Monsters in the cloister

Santa Maria, detail of a capital. At each corner of the capital, the maw of a lion is closing around the trunk of a man. This theme is also found on the façade on either side of the central doorway, and on some of the capitals of the church and cloister.

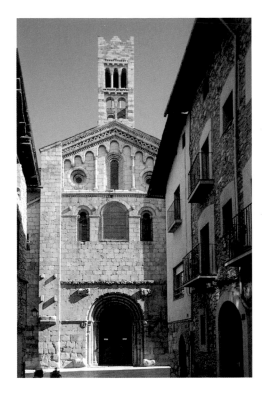

Right
A late Romanesque interior
Santa Maria, La Seu d'Urgell,
before 1131–1180, view from the
south aisle. The nave is covered
with a barrel vault on transverse
ribs and the aisles by groin vaults.
The massive pillars display nook-
shafts. The pillars rise from a
torus; their edges are chamfered
and studded with ball decoration
in relief.

In Catalonia, the architecture of the twelfth century developed naturally out of the first Romanesque. The cathedrals of Vic, Lleida, Barcelona, Gerona and Tarragona, and the urban monasteries of Sant Pau del Camp (San Pablo del Campo) in Barcelona and Sant Pere (San Pedro) de Galligans in Gerona, were built or rebuilt. The cathedral of Santa Maria at La Seu d'Urgell, begun before 1131, seems closest to the building tradition of the first Romanesque. (An Italian architect, Raimundus, was contracted to the cathedral chapter in 1175.) Features testifying to foreign influence can often be detected in buildings otherwise typical of the Catalan tradition. Thus the churches of San Pedro in Besalú and Sant Joan de les Abadesses (San Juan de las Abadesas) show French influence, while the Gothic style is presaged in the great basilicas of Lleida, Tarragona and Sant Cugat del Vallès.

Two-storey cloisters
Sant Cugat del Vallès, cloister, twelfth century. The cloister galleries are covered with a semicircular ashlar barrel vault, whose thrust is compensated for by the thickness of the walls and the stepped buttresses. These project only slightly at capital height, and extend into the upper part of the wall between the blind arcades resting on corbels. The latter run beneath a cornice, which must once have supported a roof.

A Pyrenean cloister
Santa Maria, La Seu d'Urgell, before 1131–1180, cloister. Situated to the south of the cathedral, the rectangular cloister has lost one of its four original galleries. The original arcades are set on single columns, with piers at the corners. The upper part of the wall is invisible behind the overhanging roof of timber and slate. The granite capitals are of somewhat rudimentary execution, with barely sketched foliage, and figurative scenes in which the lion theme predominates. The overall effect is reminiscent of the Romanesque cloisters of Roussillon and the Cerdagne, north of the Pyrenees.

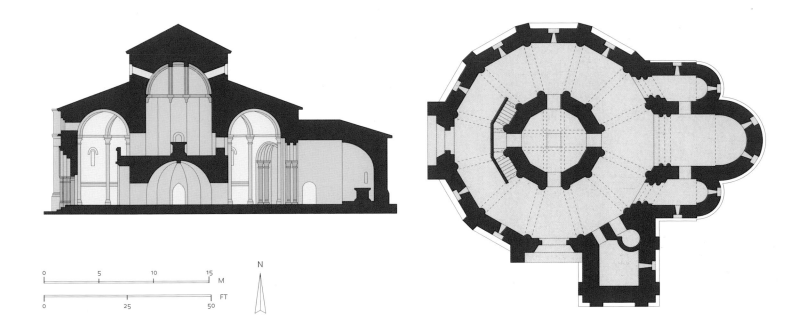

Inspired by the Holy Sepulchre
The Vera Cruz, Segovia, consecrated in 1208, longitudinal section and plan. Two doors with semicircular arches lead into the building, at the centre of which is a polygonal chapel. The annular ambulatory surrounds this twelve-sided polygon. There is a tripartite echelon apse. The bell-tower is a later addition. The building symbolically reflects the Church of the Holy Sepulchre in Jerusalem.

The annular nave
The Vera Cruz, Segovia, interior. The twelve-sided chapel in the centre of the building is in two storeys. Four openings with pointed arches lead into it. Columns with sculpted capitals carry the ribs of the vault. Between them, the wall surface is decorated with a blind arcade of slightly pointed arches.

Castilian ornamentation
Santo Domingo, Silos, detail of a
cloister capital, late twelfth
century. The abacus of the double
capital remains square for half its
height. Then the parts of the
capital divide to follow the shaft.
The sculpted ornament represents
paired animals in combat.
Addorsed lions, interwoven with
plant stems, contort their necks to
come head to head. The delicate
carving, the sinuous outlines and
the perfect symmetry of the
composition all testify to the
talents of the Castilian sculptors.

**Origin and end of Castilian
Romanesque**
Santo Domingo, Silos, cloister.
The cloister forms an irregular
quadrilateral, and has two storeys
of very regular semicircular
arcades. The arcades rest on
elegant twin columns mounted
on a low wall. The space between
the twinned columns varies from
gallery to gallery. The result is
wide differences among the bases
and capitals. With its harmonious
proportions and rich ornament,
Santo Domingo offers a remarkable example of Romanesque art
in Castile.

The latter, begun in late Romanesque style, was completed in the Gothic era, during the fourteenth century. Catalan Gothic treatment of rose windows is well represented by the main rosette here; in its heavy, imposing forms, tracery is emphasised at the expense of glass. Sant Cugat del Vallès also has one of the largest carved Romanesque cloisters in Catalonia. There are four galleries, whose broad bays open on to an immense lawned garth. The superlative capitals demonstrate the mastery attained by Romanesque sculptors of the late twelfth century.

In the kingdoms of León and Castile, the central plan type spread as far as Salamanca and Segovia; the church of the Vera Cruz in Segovia (circa 1208) offers a remarkable two-storey example. San Vicente in Ávila, by contrast, proves that Burgundian influence reached as far as Castile. The first campaign of construction produced a plan similar to that of San Isidoro in León: a nave of four bays giving on to a projecting transept with three parallel apses. In the second campaign two further bays were added to the nave, which also received tribunes and ribbed vaults. At the west end is a porch with two towers reminiscent of the monumental narthexes of

A palace façade

Santo Domingo, Soria, late twelfth century, façade. The façade is wider than it is high. On either side of the central portal are two registers of blind arcades, with pairs of columns divided by pilasters. Above, a rose window is set in the triangular gable; its diameter is equal to the width of the portal. A carved cross sits on the peak of the gable. French influence is clear, but the façade remains a major work of Spanish Romanesque.

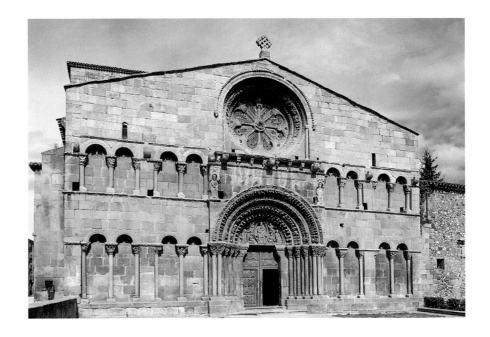

Anticipating Gothic sculpture

Santo Domingo, Soria, tympanum of the façade portal. In the centre, God the Father sits in a mandorla; on his knees is the Infant Jesus. God wears a crown and sports an immaculate beard and moustache. On either side, four angels carry the symbols of the Tetramorph: to the right the book and the lion, to the left the eagle and bull. Saint Joseph and the Virgin sit at either end. One of the four arches encompassing the tympanum presents the twenty-four elders of the Apocalypse.

Outside the walls of the city
San Vicente, Ávila, chevet, last quarter of the twelfth century. The chevet is raised over a crypt, which held the relics of Saint Vincent and his sisters. It has a tripartite echelon apse, each section of which is semicircular. Here we see the importance granted to monumental sculpture, in the form of columns with the grain of the stone laid vertically, the fine colonnettes in the window splays and the modillions beneath the roof. This wealth of ornament was to prove a characteristic of the main Romanesque churches of Castile and Aragon.

Page 165 below left
Late Romanesque sculpture
San Vicente, Ávila, Annunciation from the south portal, shortly after 1200. The angel Gabriel approaches Mary, who sits beneath a sort of arcade. This arrangement, and the supple treatment of the drapery, suggest that the still strong Romanesque tradition was already leaning towards Gothic.

Burgundy. The same influence is perceptible in the carving of the portal, which resembles those of Saint-Lazare at Avallon, Saint-Bénigne at Dijon, and Vermenton.

The cathedral of Pamplona is difficult to date with any precision. A French prelate (1082–1114) presided over its construction; it seems that this was in full swing by 1101, under the direction of an architect named Stephen, who was simultaneously responsible for the building work at Santiago de Compostela. After having collapsed in 1390, the cathedral was built up once more. The distinctive features of the cathedral were its projecting transept and three apses. The two lateral apses were some distance away from the central one and were semicircular outside and polygonal within; the buttressing of the apse vaults was typically French.

It is no easier to put a precise date on the construction of Santo Domingo at Silos in Castile. The church and oldest part of the cloister (the eastern and northern galleries) would seem to be eleventh century. Grimaldus, who wrote his *Vita Dominici Siliensis* (Life of Domingo of Silos) between 1088 and 1109, speaks of the building being completely reconstructed. He also states that, in 1073, the body of Saint Domingo was buried at the cloister door to the church. Some years later, probably in 1076, his remains were translated into the church, where they were interred before the altar of Saint Martin. The research of I. Bango Torviso and J. Williams seems to prove that the 1088 consecration was of the lower, and not, as had been

Well-structured architecture
San Vicente, Ávila, last quarter of the twelfth century, plan. A first building campaign (1190) produced the three semicircular chapels of the chevet, the transept, and the four last bays of the nave. Later, the nave was extended by a further two bays, the aisles received tribunes, and a porch framed by two towers was constructed at the east end. The porch displays a perfect ribbed vault, but its main importance lies in its great sculpted portal, which is reminiscent of the Burgundian portals of the second half of the twelfth century.

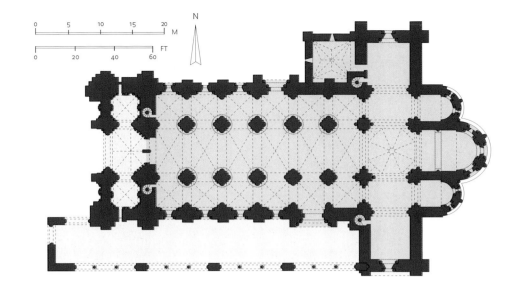

Ornamental springing line
San Vicente, Ávila. The nave is rib-vaulted; the diagonal ribs spring from the capitals of the half-columns engaged in the piers.

thought, of the upper church. This is taken to prove that the cloister was built after the death of the saint. The carved capitals in the south arm of the transept of the upper church are thought to show that this part of the building, which includes the portal of the Virgin, is of a later style; Peter Klein dates it to 1120–1130.

Rural buildings in Castile display clear links with the Islamic world, especially in their ornamentation. This is the case, for example, with the baldaquins and cloister arcades of San Juan de Duero in Soria. Similar arcades can be found in Amalfi, in southern Italy, and in Sicily. Entrance porticoes are also characteristic of this kind of architecture; they form a covered, porticoed gallery, and sometimes accommodate tombs, as in San Isidoro at León. The particular function they served was as a meeting-place for the laity (San Estebán in Gormaz, Sepúlveda, San Miguel and Nuestra Señora at Rivero, and Rebolledo de la Torre). This architecture was in every sense an outgrowth of the everyday life of the Romanesque era.

One product of the meeting of East and West in Spain was the *cimborio*. These very individual domes are found, for example, at the crossings of the cathedrals of Salamanca and Zamora. Salamanca cathedral is on the same plan as San Isidoro at León and San Vicente at Ávila: a projecting transept opening on to three semicircular apses, each of which is preceded by an orthogonal bay and vaulted with a semi-dome. Since construction began in 1150 and lasted for some seventy-five years, the influence of Gothic architecture is strongly felt here. Ribbed vaults replaced the Romanesque barrel vault in the transept and were used to roof the nave and side-aisles. The lantern tower at the crossing is generally referred to as the Torre del Gallo ('Tower of the

The *cimborio*
Old Cathedral, Salamanca, second half of twelfth century, interior of the dome. The circular drum is mounted on pendentives and pierced with two superposed rows of windows. The dome itself sits on this massive base, and comprises sixteen webs defined by ribs that meet at the central boss. This lantern tower, called the Torre del Gallo ('Tower of the Cock'), is the most famous of the Spanish *cimborios*.

Ornament underlining structure
Zamora cathedral, second half of the twelfth century, interior of the dome above the crossing. The dome rests on a circular drum mounted on pendentives and lit by a single row of windows. The sixteen concave webs are underlined by the coloured zig-zag decoration of the ribs.

The exterior of the *cimborio* at Zamora
The ribs of the dome are emphasised by the crests. Little circular lantern towers alternate with very narrow pediments. The intricate arrangement and decoration of this *cimborio* offer many points of affinity with architecture in west France.

Cock'). It comprises a circular drum on pendentives, and is pierced with two rows of windows similar to the tower of the collegiate church of Santa María la Mayor in Toro.

The dome of the Catedral Vieja (Old Cathedral) in Salamanca has, at least externally, certain affinities with Limousin bell-towers: corner lantern turrets alternate with very elongated gables, and the overall form is rather tall and narrow. It bears comparison with the dome of Zamora cathedral, which, however, derives largely from Byzantine models. Building began in 1151 and was almost finished by 1174; the Gothic influence is consequently less marked. Only the nave of the Old Cathedral is rib-vaulted; the transept has a barrel-vaulted roof and the side-aisles are groin-vaulted. At the crossing, a circular drum on pendentives carries a dome consisting of sixteen concave gores underpinned by ribs that meet in a central boss; the ribs have a chevron decoration. Unlike Salamanca, the drum in the dome of Zamora is pierced with only one row of windows.

A fortified cathedral
Coimbra cathedral, façade, late twelfth century. The façade is framed by two powerful buttresses, which rise without ornament to the roof. A central projecting section contains a particularly deep portal and window, both of them with multiple archivolts resting on columns with capitals. Windows flanked by blind arcades reflect the level of the tribune within. The crenellated parapet crowns the walls, while the little windows of the ground floor resemble loopholes; the whole effect is rather of a fortress than of a cathedral.

Tranquil rhythms
Coimbra cathedral, cloister, late twelfth century. The cloister has four galleries opening through five slightly pointed arches; each of these spans twin semicircular arches, carried on very narrow columns. Above the arcades are oculi decorated with simple geometrical motifs. The inter-mediary supports, reinforced on the outside by powerful buttresses, carry the transverse ribs of the gallery rib vault. The cusped abacuses and the triple convex mouldings on the intrados of the arches alternate light and shade and enhance the elegance of the whole.

Right
Brick replaces stone
Évora cathedral, Portugal, late
twelfth century, interior. The
cathedral is on a cruciform plan.
The nave and transept present a
pointed barrel vault. The nave is
divided into seven bays by piers
with engaged columns. Above the
pointed arches of the arcade, a
further series of arcades is found
in each bay at tribune level. The
entire building is in brick.

**An irregular and transitional
construction**
Évora cathedral, exterior from the
cloister. Sturdy buttresses are
placed at regular intervals along
the cathedral walls, which are
pierced with double windows
displaying slightly pointed arches.
The roof is flat, and bristles with
crenellations. The pointed arches
of the cloister galleries are
surmounted by oculi with
ornamentation akin to mudejar
art, which spread through Europe
in the twelfth century. This
architecture has as many Gothic as
Romanesque features, and is
transitional in style.

In Galicia and Portugal, the influence of Santiago de Compostela was very widespread; it can be seen in the cathedrals of Lugo, Orense, Tuy and Coimbra. The last-named is vaulted throughout; it is of basilican plan, and has a projecting transept with apsidioles and a chevet without ambulatory. The two-storey elevation of the nave with its tribune galleries resembles that of Santiago. This arrangement is also found in Lisbon cathedral. A good number of the smaller churches of northern Portugal have only a single nave, which extends into a rectangular apse of pre-Romanesque tradition, and are timber-roofed. By contrast, the cathedral of Évora, whose elevation comprises a false triforium and whose pointed barrel vault remains thoroughly Romanesque in tradition, clearly presages the development of Gothic architecture.

The Relation between Architecture and Ornament

Romanesque churches were generally poly-chrome. It is a little-known fact that in the Middle Ages a church was incomplete until painted decoration had been applied, or, at the very least, a revetment imitating stonemasonry. Like the churches of late antiquity and the Carolingian period, Romanesque churches were given a rich iconographical decoration; this was true even before sculpted decoration became conventional. Naves generally bore narrative cycles, while the visionary composition built up on the apse often influenced the programme of the façade sculptures.

Painting is no less important than sculpture to our understanding of the Romanesque church. On the walls, iconographic programmes allowed the fundamental principles of Christianity and the feudal social order to be communicated to the faithful. The vision of God presented on the intrados of the apse was generally a *Maiestas Domini*, a Christ enthroned in Majesty and offering His blessing, surrounded by the Elders of the Apocalypse, the symbols of the Evangelists, and archangels or seraphim. Sometimes the *Maiestas Domini* is replaced by a *Maiestas Mariae*, the Virgin and Child seated on a 'Throne of Wisdom' within a mandorla. Sometimes, Mary is depicted in the scene of the Adoration of the

Magi (Epiphany), emphasising her role in the mysteries of the Incarnation and Salvation.

The historiated cloister dates from shortly after the beginning of the twelfth century, when the desire was felt throughout the West to ornament the façades of religious buildings with monumental sculpture. This was not, in a sense, a Romanesque innovation. A similar aspiration had been evident since paleo-Christian times, and was manifested in basilican architecture (Old Saint Peter's in Rome, Porec in Croatia): the desire to create a monumental façade through pictorial techniques such as painting and mosaic. And Romanesque artists made symbolic use of classical models when, at the entrance to the New Jerusalem, that is, the Church, they constructed veritable triumphal arches or evocations of city gates. This enrichment of the façade became gradually more intense, and reached its culmination late in the Romanesque period, in the second half of the twelfth century.

Between the façade and the apse, the Romanesque church interior featured a decorative scheme partly consisting of painting, as defined above. But we must complete this account with a description of the figurative carving of the capitals. In the nave, narrative progression was the norm. Elsewhere, groups of capitals were

Left
The art of wall painting
Sant Pere del Burgal, detail of a fresco, first quarter of the twelfth century. This painting belongs to the Pedret school and shows Saint John the Baptist and the apostle Paul. (Museu Nacional d'Art de Catalunya, Barcelona)

Centre
The technique of mosaics
Murano, detail of a mosaic floor, 1141. This example is in *opus tessellatum*, made of *tesserae* (cubes between 1 and 2 cm²) of stone, brick, marble and *pâte de verre*, and shows two birds, one on either side of a vase.

Right
Sculpture in polychrome wood
The so-called *Majestat Batlló*, from Olot, Catalonia, mid-twelfth century. Height: 96 cm. Christ wears a long tunic tied at the waist. His hair and beard are thick, and He wears an imposingly majestic air. (Museu Nacional d'Art de Catalunya, Barcelona)

Left

The art of illuminated manuscripts in northern Spain

Liber Testamentorum (Book of Testaments), circa 1118. In the centre is Saint Bertin enthroned, holding a crozier in his right hand and extending the left to receive the book offered to him by Abbott Odbert. (Oviedo, Cathedral Archive)

Above right

The Creation Tapestry

Detail late eleventh – early twelfth century, linen, 4.55 m x 3.45 m. A young, beardless Christ at the centre orders the Creation of the Universe. (Museu de la Catedral, Gerona)

Below right

Painted vaults

Saint-Savin-sur-Gartempe, Construction of the Tower of Babel from the nave roof, early twelfth century. Christ addresses the builders while Nimrod lifts blocks of stone up to the masons. The composition can be easily read from a distance.

intended for specific parts of the church. The ambulatory and choir received the themes of the Passion and Resurrection, sometimes accompanied by the Public Life, Apocalypse and Last Judgment. No general rule governs the arrangement of sculptures inside the church; but the nave was often decorated with carvings representing Salvation, the lives of the saints, and typological correspondences between the Old and New Testaments.

To understand the relation between architecture and decoration, we must also take into account the relation of painted and carved decoration with church furniture: baldaquin, choir-screen, ambo and Paschal candelabra (in Italy all these were carved in stone) and the wooden antepedia and sculptures of Christ, Mary, or the Descent from the Cross found throughout western Europe.

The Virgin, seated squarely full-face with the Child on her knees, is perhaps the most characteristic image of Romanesque sculpture. The representation of Mary as the Throne of the Wisdom of the Father encapsulated the doctrine of the Incarnation; her rigid expression slowly evolved until, by the late twelfth century, she also conveyed the tenderness of mother and child.

These statues might be placed on an altar, and could be carried during a procession. This was also done with wooden sculptures of Christ; He is generally represented alive on the Cross, dressed in a long tunic or a loin-cloth. Among the repertory of wooden carvings, the Descent from the Cross was the most spectacular and dramatic example of wooden furniture to be seen in the church. Such groups were associated with the sacred representations of the Easter period, and might occupy different parts of the nave; they might also be suspended above the entrance or above the screen separating the clergy from the congregation, where they were still more theatrical in effect.

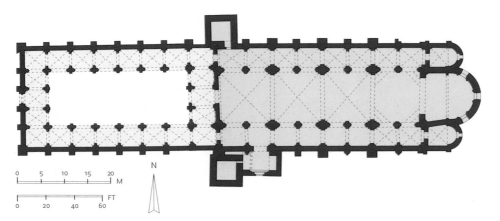

The paleo-Christian formula
Sant'Ambrogio, Milan, after 1174, plan. The church is preceded by a vast porticoed atrium. The nave is divided into three sections of square plan with bulbous rib vaults. It opens directly on to the chevet with its tripartite apse. At the crossing is a dome on squinches, beneath which is a ciborium. This is a perfect example of Lombard Romanesque.

Italy

Italy was politically fragmented during the Romanesque era, and its architecture reflects these divisions in many regional styles. Subject to western European, Oriental and southern influences, Italy was a land rich in experience and invention. Innovation was stimulated by those two specifically Italian features, the inspiration of classical tradition and the reuse of classical *spolia*. In several regions we encounter widespread use of brick (not to the exclusion of stone), large, vaulted naves, and an abundance of mural decoration.

In northern Italy a tradition of sober architecture developed; here the influence of southern France was a constant factor. Lombard Romanesque was both nourished and constrained by an uninterrupted architectural tradition going back to Roman and paleo-Christian epochs, which included the monuments of Ravenna. At Como, the church of Sant'Abbondio (consecrated in 1095) presents a nave with four aisles, a timber roof and a generously proportioned choir. The influence of the first Romanesque is visible in the small stones of which it is built, the external blind arcading and the two square-plan bell-towers. Sant'Abbondio served as a model for San Giacomo in Como, and the now ruined Sant'Eufemia on the island of Comacina.

The monastery church of Sant'Ambrogio in Milan (after 1174) also adopts a basilican plan, with a nave and side-aisles. There is no transept, and the nave leads directly to the chevet with its three semicircular apses. Its continuity with the paleo-Christian heritage is clear in the atrium by which it is preceded. The elevation with

Below left
The atrium and façade
Sant'Ambrogio, Milan. The portico of the rectangular atrium features composite piers. The lower part of the façade is formed by one of the galleries of the atrium, above which the arcades of the tribune bring light into the nave. On either side are bell-towers decorated with Lombard bands.

Right
Stucco furnishings
Sant'Ambrogio, Milan, detail of the ciborium, tenth century. It is raised on four Roman porphyry columns and has four trapezoidal faces, each containing a scene with three polychrome stucco figures. Facing the entrance is Christ handing the Law to Saints Peter and Paul.

An imposing interior

San Michele, Pavia, consecrated in 1155, interior. The massive clustered piers define the structure of the nave; the particularly ornate capitals carry large moulded arches, which are repeated at tribune level.

A compact building

San Michele, Pavia, plan. The broad nave and aisles lead to imposing transepts, choir and apse. At the crossing is a lantern tower on squinches. In the fifteenth century, the nave received a rib vault of oblong plan.

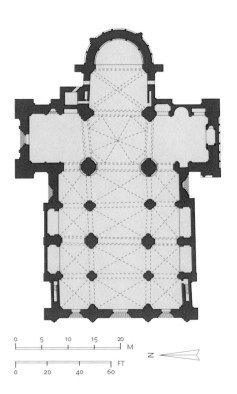

Page 174

A massive ornate chevet

Modena cathedral, begun circa 1099, chevet. The arms of the transept attain the same height as the choir, which ends in three semicircular chapels. The choir is raised over a crypt. Above it two slender turrets present an arcaded opening in their upper storey. This ornamental motif also runs around the three chapels of the apse, creating a very elegant composition.

The openings of the west façade

Modena cathedral, façade. The body of the façade is framed by powerful buttresses. The porch is surmounted by a loggia, above which is a wide rose window dating from the late twelfth century. The wall surfaces are animated by the arcades of a gallery with triple bays. The overall effect is of striking contrasts of light and shade. This type of façade inspired most of the constructions in the Po valley between the twelfth and thirteenth centuries.

Emilian Romanesque exemplified

Modena cathedral, plan. The building has nave and side aisles; there is no transept, and the nave leads directly into the deep choir with its tripartite apse. The Royal Portal on the south side and the famous Ghirlandina Tower date from the late twelfth century. The crypt extends beneath the nave and aisles of the choir.

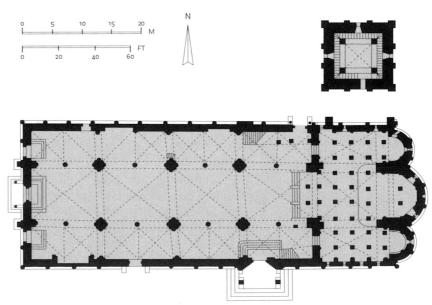

tribunes and the ribbed vaulting found almost throughout the building, on the other hand, presage new developments in Romanesque architecture. These are also found in San Michele at Pavia, though there, in addition, we find a spacious transept and a raised choir. One feature of San Michele, the wide, square-edged vaulting ribs, quickly spread throughout northern Italy. The combination of these architectural features influenced other Pavian buildings: San Pietro in Ciel d'Oro, San Teodoro and San Lazzaro, in addition to San Stefano and Santa Maria del Popolo, which have since been destroyed.

The strong links between Lombardy and Emilia are clearly perceptible in the cathedral of Modena (begun circa 1099). Here again nave and side-aisles lead through a non-projecting transept to three semicircular apses; yet again, alternating columns and piers form tripartite bays like tribune bays, but open directly on to the side-aisles. The construction of Parma cathedral (begun 1096) is almost contemporary with that of Modena; its original feature is the chevet, which is raised on a high crypt, like that of Speyer. The projecting transept has two apsidioles on each of its arms, one facing along the axis of the transept, the other facing east. The

The pattern of the north Italian screen-façade
Modena cathedral, begun circa 1099, detail of external decoration. The walls of the façade and aisles and the outside of the chevet are decorated with very tall blind arcades, within which, at three-quarter height, is a row of little arches. These latter separate the lower level of the façade, with its windows, from the upper level, with its elegant gallery of triple arcades on colonnettes. The rich decoration of Modena cathedral inspired many other Emilian churches.

Above right
Coordination of interior and exterior
Modena cathedral, interior. The interior is articulated by the alternation of classical columns and the clustered pilasters that carry the rib vault of the nave.

Below right
The work of Master Wiligelmo
Modena cathedral, detail of the ornament of the transept portal. The knot created in the slender colonnette testifies to the quality of Romanesque carving in Italy; one of the earliest such sculptors was Wiligelmo of Modena.

rectangular choir has a semicircular apse. An octagonal lantern stands over the crossing. The external decoration consists of blind arcades and arcaded galleries. Once more we find the three-storey elevation and the oblong ribbed vault, though only in the nave; the side-aisles are groin-vaulted.

These churches are often accompanied by a detached bell-tower and a monumental baptistery. Northern Italy has many baptisteries from this period, for example those at Biella, Asti and Cremona. The most remarkable is undoubtedly that of Parma (1196). It is a massive octagonal tower with a ribbed dome. The elevation is on three levels. The base, which has three large portals, is decorated on the inside with semicircular niches and on the outside with blind arcades; the central register has spur buttresses at the corners, vertical pillars, and a succession of superposed galleries; the third level is decorated with a series of arcades.

Northern Italian Romanesque displays a characteristic and original treatment of façades, of which San Michele in Pavia (consecrated in 1155) is highly representative. It is divided into three broad sections by clustered colonnettes rising the full height of the façade; its triangular gable is underlined by a parallel gallery of arcades. In each section is a door with a semicircular arch. The central section has three registers: a row of three double windows, a row of three tall single windows, and two oculi. The lateral sections each have one double window. In the façade, the position of carved ornament is not subordinated to the architecture; animal friezes are inserted into the courses of stone here and there, in bands, without structural motivation. The gable arcade and windows recur in the façade of the cathedral at Parma (1076–1106). There, two horizontal rows of triple bays run across the façade, and a gallery runs under and parallel to the gable. In the centre, a two-storey porch rests on pillars, which rise from a base with sculpted lions. This type of porch gained wide currency.

In central Italy, ornament runs riot, sometimes to the detriment of the architecture. There are also considerable local differences, as for example between the monuments of Pisa and those of Florence. A feature found in the architecture of the Roman Empire is often encountered in central Italy: a white marble revetment with horizontal bands and ornamental motifs in dark green marble. This technique is found only here. As external decoration, it was combined with galleries and blind arcades, giving a sumptuous inlay effect, very different from the simple, austere paleo-Christian exteriors.

Below left
Tuscan marble
Baptistery, Pisa, begun 1152. The ground floor is decorated with tall blind arcades, the first floor with an arcaded gallery, and the second with cusped windows. The statuettes of saints and prophets were added in the mid-thirteenth century.

Below right
The celebrated Leaning Tower
The bell-tower, Pisa, 1173. This cylindrical tower is famous for the angle at which subsidence has caused it to lean. It has seven storeys plus the bell-storey, which was added in the mid-fourteenth century.

The elegance of the Pisan blind arcade

Pisa cathedral, consecrated 1118, overall view. The decoration defines the three parts of the building: aisles, tribunes and nave are identified by a storey of blind arcades, a row of pilasters and a second register of arcades respectively. The decoration is enhanced by polychrome veneering. Three doors mark the façade, which presents four loggia galleries on fine colonnettes above the blind arcades of the ground floor. The superlative complex of the Piazza dei Miracoli, with the Campo Santo on the left, ensured the renown of the Pisan style.

Tuscany remained faithful to its classical heritage throughout the Middle Ages. The architects of Pisa introduced a number of innovations, which are perfectly illustrated in the complex constituted by the cathedral, baptistery, campanile (the 'Leaning Tower') and the Campo Santo or cemetery. The cathedral was consecrated in 1118, though still unfinished. Its plan is a Latin cross with nave and four aisles opening on to a strongly projecting low transept, which itself has aisles; there is a dome at the crossing. The external decoration in marble is truly remarkable. Between apse and façade, it is arranged on three registers defined by cornices that outline the main features of the building: aisles, tribunes and nave. There is first a series of tall blind arcades, then a storey of pilasters, then a further series of blind arcades. The finishing touch is provided by rose windows and polychrome marble veneering. The register of arcades continues around the west façade, where it is pierced with three portals. Above these, four galleries of loggias are carried on slender colonnettes. This decorative scheme was much admired in Tuscany. Pisan-style galleries are found on the façades of San Michele at Lucca, San Bartolomeo in Pantano at Pistoia, and Santa Maria della Pieve at Arezzo.

The baptistery in Pisa, designed by Diotisalvi in 1152, is circular in plan. Its ornamentation matches that of the cathedral. It presents a kind of two-storey ambulatory, whose vaults rest alternately on piers and columns. Gothic ornament

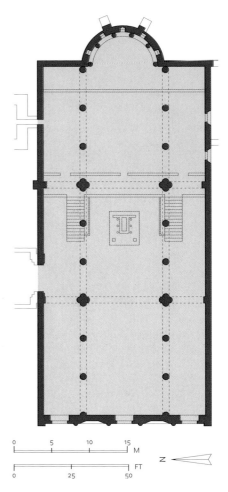

Page 181
Abstract motifs and patterns
San Miniato al Monte, Florence, completed circa 1150, looking west. Inlaid green and white marble emphasises the forms of the arcades, and entirely covers the walls with abstract linear compositions.

The survival of the basilican tradition
San Miniato al Monte, Florence, completed circa 1150, interior and plan. The rhythms of the nave are defined by the alternation of columns and piers with engaged columns; the latter carry the diaphragm arches on which the timber roof is supported. The choir is raised above a groin-vaulted crypt space. It is unusually deep, and ends in a semicircular apse.

was added in the thirteenth century; the dome dates from the fourteenth century. The campanile is the work of Bonanno; it is a cylindrical tower decorated with arcaded galleries in the manner of the cathedral. The complex is completed by the Campo Santo, a rectangular courtyard with blind arcades on the outside and porticoed within, and set within a walled precinct.

Most of the churches in Pisa take their inspiration from these architectural and decorative models, notably San Frediano and San Paolo a Ripa d'Arno. The model was also followed in the islands and ports under Pisan domination. The basilica of San Gavino at Porto Torres in Sardinia is a good illustration of this; it has a double apse and alternating supports and is richly ornamented. San Gavino in its turn inspired other monuments, such as Santa Maria at Silanus and Santa Giusta at Oristano.

Florentine Romanesque explored a different kind of ornament, based on poly-chrome marble veneering and the use of classical *spolia*. The church of San Miniato al Monte (completed circa 1150) is a perfect example of this. It is a basilica with nave and side-aisles; its very rhythmic nave displays a succession of columns interrupted

by piers with engaged columns. The timber roof is supported on diaphragm arches. The choir is deep and raised high above the nave by a crypt only slightly below nave level. The decoration of the façade shows a characteristic play of white and green marble. The lower register has blind arcades with semicircular arches framing linear polychrome compositions, two of which convey the impression of lateral doors. Above this, compositions of lines and circles are set on either side of a window. The façade is topped by a pediment decorated with the same motifs on a smaller scale. This decorative scheme inspired the façade of the Badia at Fiesole near Florence. It reached perfection in the baptistery in Florence, which is entirely covered, inside and out, with green and white marble veneering.

Other central Italian buildings show the influence of Cluny, such as the abbey church of Sant'Antimo, which has a choir with radiating chapels. Most of the churches of Spoleto and the cathedral at Todi are more akin to Lombard models; by contrast, the Tuscan basilican plan is found in the cathedrals of Spoleto, Narni and Assisi. But many buildings in this area came under the precocious influence of Gothic, one such being the church of San Francesco in Assisi, whose construction began in 1228 on Gothic lines.

Rome and the region of Latium, though influenced by northern Italy, maintained the paleo-Christian basilican plan. An atrium precedes the façade of the church of Santi Quattro Coronati. A colonnaded portico precedes the façade of San Clemente. The west section of Santa Maria in Cosmedin, composed of a narthex, a

An Apulian façade
San Nicola, Bari, 1197, façade. It is divided into three sections by elegant buttresses carried on columns. The walls are pierced with single and double bays. A blind arcade follows the roof line, and the three doors are set in a web of blind arcades in low relief. Powerful quadrangular towers frame the façade, which is essentially Lombard in character.

A harmonious balance of façade and tower

Trani cathedral, façade, after 1098. The rose window is surrounded by animal carvings; below it are three windows. The ornate main portal is flanked by a row of lower, blind arcades. The elegant bell-tower is raised on tall, pointed arches. It features five storeys of ogee windows.

Sobriety and verticality

Trani Cathedral, chevet. The nave and aisles open on to a barely projecting transept leading into the three tall chapels of the apse. The central chapel presents a large window decorated with sculpted motifs. The otherwise bare surface of the wall is animated by many narrow openings. Modillions underline the cornice at roof-level on this very austere chevet.

portico and a square bell-tower, derives directly from pre-medieval buildings in Rome. Santa Maria in Trastevere has the classical ornament of arcades and pilaster strips. Only the campaniles, such as the ones of San Crisogomo and Santa Maria in Cosmedin with their series of openings, reflect the new architectural formulas.

In Apulia, Calabria and sometimes even in Campania, the mixture of styles is determined by Norman, Oriental and classical influences. A basilican plan is found at Carinola and Sessa Aurunca, and in the cathedrals of Salerno and Capua in the region of Campania. Southern Italy reflects the influence of Arab art, as the cloister at Amalfi testifies: its slender columns carry arches intersecting in threes. This form of decoration is also found in the bell-towers there and at Gaeta. The buildings of Ravello also manifest Islamic influence. By contrast, in Apulia and Calabria, it is Byzantine influence that predominates. Canosa cathedral in Apulia (consecrated in

Roman inlaid marble
Santa Maria in Cosmedin, Rome, twelfth century, interior. The alterations made by Calixtus II conserved the essential elements of the paleo-Christian tradition in both plan and ornament. The liturgical furnishing is unusually complete, with a baldaquin dating from the late thirteenth or early fourteenth century, signed by Deodatus, who worked in the Cosmati style.

Page 185 below
Cosmati work
San Clemente, Rome, twelfth century, interior of nave. The building is of paleo-Christian basilican plan, with nave and aisles separated by sets of four classical columns alternating with large piers. The apse is tripartite. The centre of the nave is occupied by the *schola cantorum* with its two ambones and its paschal candlestick. The floor is decorated with discs of porphyry and serpentine framed by panels of geometrical motifs. These are characteristic of an art unique to Italy, the Cosmatiwork pavement.

1101) has a Latin-cross plan and five domes. In Calabria, square and Greek-cross plans, such as those of San Marco at Rossano and San Giovanni, called La Cattolica at Stilo, are common. But the influence of northern Romanesque is felt in the ambulatories with radiating chapels at Venosa, Acerenza and Aversa. A fully developed choir, typical of Norman churches such as that of Bernay, makes its appearance in Santa Maria della Roccella near Squillace. These architectural features are accompanied by a very specific form of ornament, such as the interlocking arcades already cited at Amalfi and found in San Giovanni at Stilo and San Pietro di Agro. This ornamental feature is also found in Durham cathedral in England.

Mosaic splendour on a gold background

San Clemente, Rome, mosaic of the Triumph of the Cross. The apse area is covered in mosaics dating from the first half of the twelfth century. In the centre is Christ on the cross, surrounded by twelve doves representing the Apostles. To the right and left stand Mary and Saint John. All around is a pattern of acanthus leaves forming volutes around the Crucifixion.

Sicily and Venice

Sicily, which underwent Byzantine, Arab and Norman occupation, displays an enormous architectural diversity. The patronage of Roger II and his son Guillaume I bestowed a number of remarkable buildings on the island. Many Arab stone buildings survive in the western region; in the eastern part, brick predominates. The patronage of the Norman kings of Sicily was devoted above all to the courtly architecture of Palermo. The Palatine Chapel, built by Roger II in 1132 and consecrated in about 1140, exemplifies this. Its basilican plan comprises a non-projecting transept and two apsidal chapels. The raised, pointed arches of the arcade are echoed in those supporting the dome on squinches at the chevet, and in the entrances to apse and apsidioles. The nave is considerably wider than the aisles, and is covered with a remarkable timber roof of Islamic inspiration decorated with stalactite work. The chapel is decorated throughout with mosaics revealing Byzantine as well as local influences, the latter of inferior craftsmanship.

When the *comté* became a kingdom, prestigious buildings were constructed to reflect its new status. In 1131, construction of the cathedral at Cefalù began. It has a nave and side-aisles, a projecting transept, and a very deep tripartite apse. The west façade consists of a porch flanked by two sturdy towers. This pattern is also

Mosaic decoration, Byzantine influence
Monreale cathedral, Sicily, late twelfth century, nave. The plan of the cathedral presents a basilican nave and a Greek-cross choir. Polychrome marble decorates the floor and the lower part of the walls. The mosaic decoration ornaments the upper part of the walls. The nave mosaics present scenes from Genesis. The older mosaics of the apse depict a Pantocrator above a Virgin and Child surrounded by archangels and Apostles.

An exquisitely decorated cloister
Monreale cathedral, Sicily,
cloister, late twelfth century.
Right: The columns carry pointed
arches, whose mouldings project
slightly from the abacuses. The
foliage and masks on the capitals
are very varied, as are those of the
abacuses.
Left: The decoration consists of
polychrome inlays and chevron
and chequered mosaics. The
quality of the ornament testifies
to the mastery of sculptors and
marble-workers alike.

found at Monreale cathedral, which has a particularly spacious and deep transept opening on to a tripartite chevet. The apses are vaulted. Monreale possesses a wealth of decoration. The interior is partly veneered with polychrome marble, but its principal feature is its mosaics, whose surface area exceeds 6300 m². On the outside of the chevet are tall, pointed, interlocking blind arcades in three registers. The two upper registers are enriched with colonnettes, and the decoration is completed by incrustations. The cloister adjoining the south aisle offers remarkable examples of Romanesque carving. Monreale brings together several characteristics of late Romanesque in Sicily: its plan shows the influence of northern Romanesque, the external decoration shows Islamic influence, while the mosaic decoration of the interior faithfully adheres to Byzantine tradition.

There were close connections between Sicily and such buildings in Campania as Amalfi, Salerno and Caserta Vecchia; these are obvious in the elevations and in common features such as central plans with domes, decoration in the form of interlocking arches, and the use of polychrome marble. The tower of the Martorana at Palermo and the portal of Santa Maria degli Alemanni in Messina show signs of Provençal and Poitevin influence.

In Venice there is a similar mixture of Byzantine and Western tendencies. The cathedral of San Marco (consecrated in 1094) has a Greek-cross plan with nave and side-aisles, a transept similarly divided, and a chevet with three apses, each of which has internal niches. Byzantine tradition is respected in the choice of brick construction, the inclusion of tribune galleries and the four domes resting on pillars. The narthex has five monumental portals. Such a formula defines an architectural tradition observed throughout the Venetian lagoon, in the cathedrals of Jesolo and Torcello. This tradition reaches its fullest flowering in the cathedral of Santi Maria e Donato (completed circa 1140) at Murano. The raised choir is extended by three apses; the axial apse is very wide and was originally flanked by two lateral apses. The roof is of timber. The exterior of the building is decorated with niches and galleries.

This mixture of Lombard and Ravennate traditions is also found in Verona in the region of Veneto around the year 1000. The church of San Lorenzo has a basilican plan; its transept has axial apsidioles and opens on to a choir with two further apsidioles. Lombard bands (pilaster-strips) enliven the walls of the apse and façade of the cathedral. This kind of ornament is also found on the façade of the Benedictine church of San Zeno Maggiore. There a gallery of small blind arcades is set midway up the façade on either side of the porch, and there are two buttresses of triangular section; these support the pediment, which is separated from the rest of the façade by a plat band on modillions. The porch is surrounded by carved reliefs set flush with the wall.

Finally, Cistercian buildings are found throughout Italy. The surviving monasteries date from the late twelfth and early thirteenth centuries. Those of northern Italy are brick-built and use ribbed vaulting. They all have the same plan: nave and side-aisles, projecting transept and several flat-ended apses, the axial apse extending beyond the others. The abbeys of Chiaravalle Milanese and Chiaravalle della Colomba (both begun in about 1135) are typical of this group. The Cistercian churches of central Italy and Latium played an essential role in the development of Gothic architecture. The most famous such buildings are the abbeys of Fossanova and Casamari. They have a similar plan; the nave is separated from the aisles by cruciform piers, there is a spacious projecting transept with four lateral apsidioles, and the chevet is flat-ended. This is in most respects identical to the plan of Fontenay.

Between Byzantium and the West
Martorana, Palermo, twelfth century. On the right flank of the church stands this elegant campanile, its four storeys each set in from the one below. The splays of the double bays are adorned with slender and richly ornamented colonnettes. The highly imaginative decoration and the pointed arches suggest Arab influences.

Roman and Venetian influences
Cathedral of Santi Maria e Donato, Murano, completed circa 1140. The nave is divided by tall columns with Corinthian capitals carrying broad semicircular arcades. The structure of the church as a whole is strongly influenced by the paleo-Christian tradition. The pavement boasting stylised animals dates from the twelfth century. It is a typical example of Romanesque mosaic floors in the Venetian lagoon area.

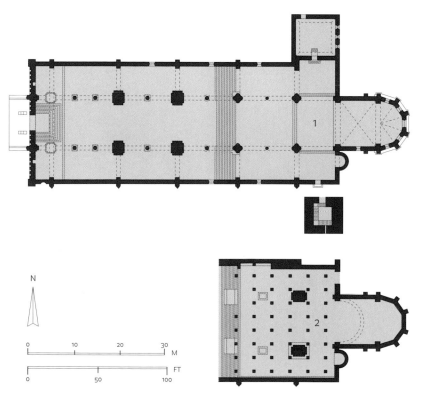

N

0   10   20   30 M

0   50   100 FT

A highly monumental west end

San Zeno Maggiore, Verona, west façade, early twelfth century. The tufa façade is divided by buttresses into three sections. The wall surface is animated with vertical bands and a gallery of arcades in the lower part. The single portal is surmounted by a baldaquin supported by columns rising from carved lions. Above the portal is an immense rose window dating from the late twelfth century.

A simple architecture

San Zeno Maggiore, Verona, plan (1) and plan of crypt (2), twelfth century. A basilican structure without transept, it has a nave and single aisles with a very deep choir set above a huge crypt. The Gothic elevation of the apse is divided into five facets.

Monumental doors

San Zeno Maggiore, Verona, bronze doors, second quarter of the twelfth century, 4.8 x 3.6 m. They are made up of forty-eight panels assembled in a wooden frame, executed by various masters. The iconography centres on the Old and New Testaments, with Apocalyptic themes and the story of Saint Zeno. Bronze doors are among the major monumental constructions of the Middle Ages, and were coveted by all major religious centres.

Right

The advent of Gothic
San Zeno Maggiore, Verona, cloister, twelfth–thirteenth century. The arcades rest on twin columns. The decorative scheme of the lateral walls is followed in the cloister, with brick arcades and tufa columns. The artistic development places this cloister at the cusp of Romanesque and Gothic.

The play of brick and tufa
San Zeno Maggiore, Verona, twelfth century, general view. The lateral walls display alternating bands of tufa and brick, which are repeated on the campanile. The rhythms of the aisle walls are created by the regular flat buttresses and the double windows with moulded arches. Above them, the buttresses are triangular in section and the bays are single. The cornices of aisle and nave are underlined by little arches. The overall effect is very pleasing.

A Varied Display

The Northern Romanesque

The shrine of Charlemagne
Silver, copper and bronze, partly gilt; enamel, jewels and cabochons. 94 cm high x 57 cm wide x 204 cm long. Aachen, between 1165 and 1215. On the front of the shrine sits Charlemagne enthroned. His face is modelled after Frederick Barbarossa, who pleaded for the canonization of Charles, which was effected in 1165. To the right and left are pope Leo III and Bishop Turpin of Reims, in the gable the Pantocrator. The shrine is a chief work of Romanesque art from the Rhine-Meuse region. (Cathedral, Aachen)

Germany

In Germany in the first half of the twelfth century the Ottonian formal language, which had especially influenced the architecture of Lower Saxony and Westphalia, was further developed and refined. Vaulting came late on the scene, appearing at different dates in different locations. Vaulted naves came very late to Lower Saxony, long after they were firmly established in the Rhineland. Construction at Freckenhorst began in the late eleventh century; the church of Sankt Bonifatius was consecrated in 1129. Its Romanesque nave is not vaulted. It has an imposingly large westwork, flanked by two towers, clearly derived from the Ottonian tradition.

Built between 1010 and 1022/1033, the Benedictine church of Sankt Michael at Hildesheim presented a regular Ottonian crossing and the alternating supports separating the nave from the aisles that remained characteristic of churches in the German principalities for at least a century. Their continued use is illustrated by Sankt Servatius in Quedlinburg and Sankt Godehard in Hildesheim, which both date from the second half of the twelfth century. In the Liebfrauenkirche (the church of Our Lady) in Halberstadt (1136) the alternation appears only in outlines, but the tower-façade is typical of the region.

The chevet of Speyer cathedral, in the upper Rhine valley, was reconstructed at the behest of Emperor Henry IV about 1095. The influence of its gallery of powerful arcades on colonnettes spread throughout the Rhineland territories. At the same time, the Benedictine abbey of Maria Laach was under construction; work had begun in 1093 under the Count Palatine Henry II, and was finished only in the thirteenth century. Towards the mid-twelfth century the nave was groin-vaulted between transverse arches. Though Maria Laach has a certain overall unity, there is a visible development from the older, east block to the later, west one, which was not finished until 1230. The east choir, raised above a groin-vaulted crypt, is square in plan and comprises a single orthogonal bay; on it rests an inclined groin vault. Preceding the semicircular apse, the choir is flanked, as at Speyer, by two tall square bell-towers. At the crossing rises a low, wide, octagonal tower. This was counterbalanced at the west end, where the need was felt to 'modernise'; the narrower transept has slender stair turrets at the end of each arm, and a massive square tower rises over the crossing. Despite this abundance of outward features, the whole has a certain austerity. Ornament is confined to the use of polychrome stone: red and grey sandstone, white and yellow limestone, and blue basalt. There are Lombard bands on the nave walls, apses and bell-towers, but the tall blind arcades so often encountered in twelfth-century Rhineland architecture are not found here.

Architects found it difficult to escape Ottonian formulae, as Maria Laach testifies. The cathedral of Sankt Peter at Worms, founded in the Hohenstaufen epoch, was reconstructed around 1181 at the instigation of Bishop Conrad II. Here earlier experiment found its fulfilment, yet the Ottonian heritage was maintained. The building is of Ottonian proportions – it is 138 m long – and Ottonian bipolarity. The east transept has a tower at the crossing, lateral towers, and two choirs; the east

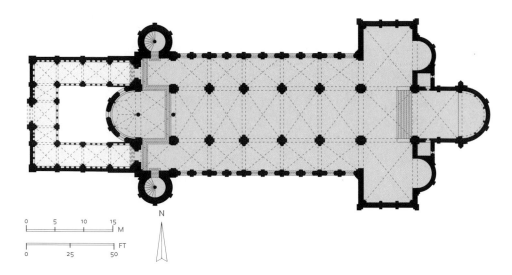

The Ottonian tradition
Maria Laach abbey, 1093– early
thirteenth century, plan. The
western apse is preceded by a
small atrium. The east choir is
elevated over a crypt and has a
single orthogonal bay and tripartite apse. The west choir has a
narrower transept opening on to a
single counter-apse, which is
flanked by two cylindrical stair
turrets. Maria Laach is typical
of twelfth-century Rhineland
architecture.

chevet is of semicircular plan inside and flat outside. The transept has a rectangular rib vault, while the dome at the crossing is carried on eight-faceted squinches. The ornament belongs to the decorative repertory of early Romanesque: blind arcading decorates the internal walls of the nave and the outside of the chevet. These forms of decoration and of vaulting are found in southern Germany, too, for example in the cathedral at Bamberg, built in the thirteenth century. It has two choirs and a west transept leading into a polygonal apse on a circular base, raised well above the nave floor. But the elevation and openings are derived from the previous cathedral, built under Henry II (1014–1024), and again testify to a heritage faithfully preserved.

The development of architecture in these regions sometimes reflects the influence of northern Italy, especially in ornamentation. Sankt Michael at Altenstadt in Bavaria offers a groin-vaulted interior with massive pillars marching down it; but the external decoration of blind arcades and the portal with its cinnamon-coloured columns are purely Italian in inspiration. The apse of the abbey church at Königslutter shows similar characteristics in its blind arcades, applied columns and figurative elements.

There were strong connections, cultural, religious and artistic, between the Rhineland and the Meuse region during the eleventh and twelfth centuries. During this period Cologne was the scene of numerous architectural undertakings. The church of Sankt Maria im Kapitol (consecrated in 1065) played a decisive role in the creation of Rhineland Romanesque. Its highly original trefoil chevet, not unlike classical central-plan buildings, has analogies with certain north Italian churches, such as San Lorenzo in Milan. Sankt Maria im Kapitol is raised above a crypt and has a groin-vaulted ambulatory. The nave has massive rectangular pillars and a two-level elevation with large flat arcades and clerestory; the rib vault was added around 1240. It is preceded by a tower comprising a porch surmounted by a tribune, framed by two very tall stair turrets. This Ottonian or Carolingian feature contrasts with the Lombard band decoration so typical of the first Romanesque.

The church of Gross Sankt Martin was all but destroyed by fire in 1150; the reconstruction was consecrated in 1172, but building went on until the mid-thirteenth century. Its trefoil choir with rounded transept arms was inspired by Sankt Maria im Kapitol, and presages the new style. It supports an imposing central tower, capped with a dome on pendentives and framed by four barrel vaults. There are four angle turrets. To lighten the masonry and direct the thrust inward, niches are cut into the very thick internal walls of the apses, a system of buttressing that is Roman in origin. The chevet leads on from a nave divided into four bays by square

Architecture of the Holy Roman Emperor

Speyer cathedral, restored plan, 1060. The cathedral comprises a westwork made up of a porch with tribunes. The nave is 15 m wide, and has only six bays, compared to the twelve bays of the aisles. The transept is articulated into three square sections; its arms have chapels hollowed out of the thickness of the walls, and there is an octagonal lantern tower at the crossing. The chevet is raised above the crypt, and the apse is flanked by two staircase turrets.

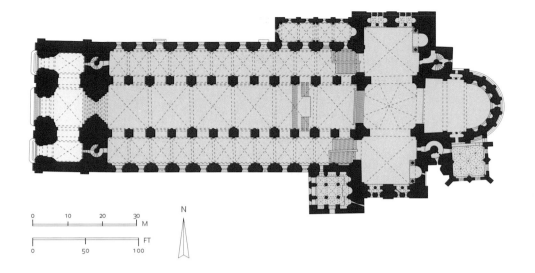

Architecture and Landscape

This view of the cathedral shows how imposing Ottonian church constructions can be – both massive and slender at the same time. With their upwardly oriented movement, the towers contrast with the choir and façade.

The marvellous towers of Speyer
Speyer cathedral, exterior of chevet. When the chevet was reconstructed after 1095, the walls of the crypt were strengthened, two bell-towers were raised where the staircase turrets had stood, and an apse was built on to the choir. The choir presents a triangular pediment underlined by a series of blind arches and niches. The apse walls are animated inside and out by large arcades with sober mouldings. The upper part of the wall is crowned with an arcaded gallery resting on slender colonnettes, which extends around the aisles and the arms of the transept.

Axiality and clear articulation
Speyer cathedral, interior of the nave. The nave was groin-vaulted in the late eleventh century; its transverse ribs combine beautifully with the direct light from the clerestory. The ribs rest on piers, every second one reinforced by dosserets and sturdy engaged columns. The alternation of supports in the double bays of the nave creates a powerful rhythmic effect. It was to be repeated in many of the great Rhineland naves.

pillars. In about 1220/1230 a rib vault of oblong plan was added to the nave, and a triforium was placed above the large arcades. On the outside of the apses, blind arcades in two registers are set above a frieze of rectangular metopes and a tall arcaded gallery. This decorative scheme became a standard feature in Rhineland architecture. Here it is completed by Lombard bands enlivening the walls of the tower and the chevet turrets.

Gross Sankt Martin was the model for Sankt Aposteln (the church of the Apostles) at Cologne, which presents the same type of trefoil chevet, but replaces Gross Sankt Martin's dome with an octagonal lantern tower carried by squinches. The central tower is flanked by two higher turrets, in observance of an Ottonian convention. The apse framed by towers gained considerable currency; fine examples are the late Romanesque churches at Neuss (Sankt Quirin), and at Roermond (church of Our Lady) and Maastricht (Sint Servaas) in today's Netherlands.

Ornamental blind bays
Speyer cathedral, interior from the crossing. The thick walls of the crossing allowed the construction of an arcaded gallery similar to that on the outside of the chevet. The decoration is completed by blind niches and oculi.

The influence of the first Romanesque is also felt in the introduction of tribunes. In Sankt Aposteln there is a series of blind niches between the arcades and the clerestory. This feature is fully developed in the two-storey apse, the upper part of which has tribune galleries.

A similar arrangement can be found in the decagon of the church of Sankt Gereon in Cologne, which was extended between 1219 and 1227. Here, tall blind arcades with pointed arches overlook a three-storey inner division, further enhancing its verticality. A row of domical vaults at ground-floor level (a remnant of the earlier construction from the fourth century) is surmounted by tribunes, which in turn carry a triforium with fan-shaped windows. Atop this third storey rises the fourth one, boasting the first plate-tracery windows found in German-speaking regions.

This formal repertory is also given an exemplary treatment in the double chapel of Sankt Maria und Klemens at Schwarzrheindorf (near Bonn). The ground plan is cruciform. Both storeys open at the east end on to an apse. In the lower church, three apses are sunk into the wall; the crossing is spanned by a groin vault with an octagonal window in the middle. The upper church has a similar ground plan, but its walls (with the exception of those on the apse) are straight. An accessible, small arcaded gallery 3.20 m high and 1.15 m wide runs around the whole structure. Its

Page 202 below
Original springing points
Speyer cathedral, detail of the supports of the nave. The columns engaged in the piers that carry the transverse ribs are interrupted by capitals at mid-height. The capitals offer a surface for decoration by vertical or chamfered undercutting. The ornament and carving technique are both typical of eleventh-century art.

A compartmented space beneath the choir
Speyer cathedral, interior of the crypt. Three arcades resting on piers flanked by engaged semi-columns divide the space into four halls. Four isolated columns create three times three bays covered by groin vaults; these display powerful transverse and wall ribs. Such compartmentalising of space is characteristic of the first Romanesque, and constitutes a break with the Ottonian tradition.

Power and authority
Worms cathedral, consecrated in 1181, chevet. The choir ends in an apse forming a five-faceted wall. It is framed by two cylindrical stair turrets whose successive storeys are clearly defined. The Lombard band decoration is akin to that of the first southern Romanesque. The upper parts of the apse present strange sculptures in the round, which serve as bases for the columns of an arcaded gallery. The superabundant sculptural decoration completes the composition.

Above left

Light floods into the crossing

Worms cathedral, consecrated in 1181, interior of the dome from the crossing. The orthogonal bay preceding the apse carries a dome of eight webs. This tower has its counterpart over the crossing of the east choir.

Above right

Animated wall surfaces

Worms cathedral. The west choir is lit by two lateral windows. The first level is decorated with blind niches, whose splayed jambs feature a series of offsets. Above these, a central rose window with radiating spokes is surrounded by polyfoil oculi.

The quest for bipolarity

Worms cathedral, plan. A westwork with two towers extends via a single orthogonal bay to a transept with a tower on squinches at the crossing. The nave, buttressed by the narrow aisles, opens on to an east massif flanked by stair turrets, and presenting one orthogonal bay leading to the polygonal apse.

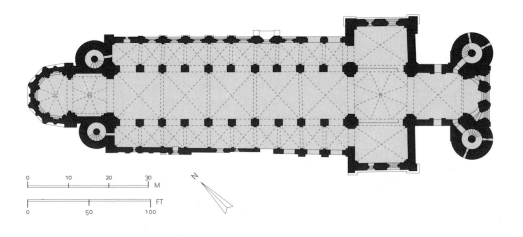

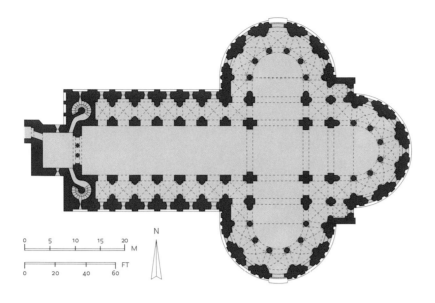

Cologne: a triple-shell termination

Sankt Maria im Kapitol, Cologne, consecrated in 1065, plan. A west tower, made up of a porch and tribune and flanked by two stair turrets, precedes the nave. This opens on to a highly original chevet in the form of a triple shell with ambulatory. This design, inspired by classical centre-planned monuments, was to play a decisive role in Rhineland Romanesque.

A simple elevation

Sankt Maria im Kapitol, Cologne, crossing and choir looking north-east. The arcades lack mouldings and are carried by sturdy rectangular pillars, some with engaged columns. Above them, the wall surface is plain up to the rose windows of the clerestory. The nave was rib-vaulted in 1240; the aisles and ambulatory of the choir are groin-vaulted.

Carved wooden doors
Sankt Maria im Kapitol, Cologne, wooden door, detail, second half of the eleventh century. This panel illustrates two New Testament scenes: the appearance of the angel to warn Joseph of the Massacre of the Innocents, and the Flight into Egypt. The juxtaposition of several episodes in a single panel, and the clarity with which the figures stand out from the background, provide clear evidence of the mastery of the Romanesque sculptors.

One of the few surviving wooden doors
Sankt Maria im Kapitol, Cologne, wooden doors. The door measures 4.3 m in height and is made up of a number of panels from (originally polychromed) wood, each with a carved frame. The scenes are from the Old and New Testaments.

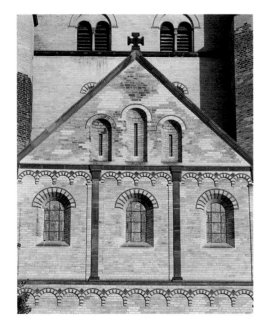

Above left

Advanced Romanesque decoration
Sankt Pantaleon, Cologne. The westwork (after 984) has tribunes above its porch. The little arches are akin to the Lombard bands of the first southern Romanesque. But here the pilasters are very different: they have bases and very simplified capitals. This form of decoration is found here for the first time north of the Alps.

Above right

An outstandingly legible interior
Sankt Pantaleon, Cologne. The westwork joins the nave via a single arcade. The choir has tribunes opening on to the nave through semicircular arcades resting on pillars. The end wall has three arches above the entrance to the church. On either side, two rows of superposed arcades permit communication between the base of the crossing tower and the arms of the transept. The austerity of the whole is softened by the use of voussoirs of alternating colour.

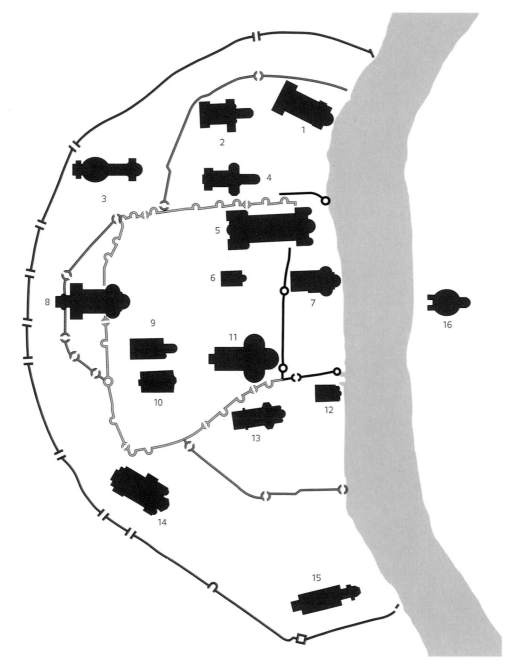

The churches of Cologne in Romanesque times
The town of Cologne played a vital role in the creation of the Rhineland style of Romanesque. Many churches were built during the second half of the twelfth century within both the Roman wall and the later city walls, which were constructed in 1106 to protect the new quarters to the north, south and west of the Roman perimeter. **1** Sankt Kunibert, **2** Sankt Ursula, **3** Sankt Gereon, **4** Sankt Andreas, **5** Cathedral, **6** Sankt Columba, **7** Gross Sankt Martin, **8** Sankt Aposteln, **9** Sankt Cäcilien, **10** Sankt Peter, **11** Sankt Maria im Kapitol, **12** Sankt Maria Lyskirchen, **13** Sankt Georg, **14** Sankt Pantaleon, **15** Sankt Severin, **16** Sankt Heribert

A synthesis of Cologne Romanesque

Sankt Aposteln (church of the Apostles), Cologne, chevet, about 1200. The chevet is organised around a lantern tower framed by octagonal turrets. The three lobes are decorated with two rows of blind arcades rising from pilasters at the first level and from semi-columns on the second level. The upper part has an arcaded gallery set above a frieze of rectangular frames, a motif also found on the walls of the tower and turrets. This handsome ensemble was inspired by Gross Sankt Martin.

arches rest on capitals with high imposts. This arrangement of the walls is reflected on the inside by the layout of the galleries and niches. The windows of the double chapel have unusual quatrefoil and fan forms, which were adopted and elaborated later on in the architecture of the Lower Rhine.

Norman buildings of the eleventh century show similar treatment of the walls above the great arcades, with tribune passages hollowed out of the walls. The point of contact would seem to be the Meuse, and in particular the cathedral of Tournai (consecrated in 1198), where the external articulation of the walls includes a register of arcades, above which is an open gallery.

The expansion of the Cistercian order into Germany and Central Europe was also a source of new buildings. Several new Cistercian monasteries were founded: at Kamp, in the Rhineland (1123), and at Altenberg near Cologne (1133), Himmerod (1134) and Eberbach (1135).

One of the best preserved and most representative examples of Cistercian architecture is the abbey at Eberbach. It has a nave and aisles and a spacious projecting transept with three aligned chapels in each arm. The chevet is square in form. The nave is spanned by a groin vault. The simple bipartite structure of the walls consists of round arcades on plain piers on the ground floor, and a clerestory lit by

Carrying the load
Sankt Aposteln, Cologne, eleventh century. A series of niches is hollowed out of the thick walls of the apse to lighten the stonework and carry the thrust of the building outwards. The rib-vaulting of the nave and the wall structure date from the reconstruction between 1192 and 1220.

two round-arched windows per bay. The lack of ornament enhances the impression of austerity that is typical of Cistercian buildings. Subsequently, the choir was enlarged, rather in the manner of Clairvaux II and Pontigny II. It became semicircular and acquired an ambulatory with radiating chapels.

The Cistercian buildings in Germany were influenced by local tendencies and in particular those of Cologne and the Rhine valley. They long remained faithful to the Romanesque canon; the Cistercian abbey church at Heisterbach near Bonn, of which only the choir has survived as a ruin, dates from the early thirteenth century and clearly illustrates this. There too we find a two-storey elevation and steeply inclined groined vaults in the nave.

Page 211 above
Lightening the supports
Cistercian abbey church of Sankt Maria, Eberbach, before 1178–1186, view from the choir looking west. The nave is divided into five and a half double bays by powerful pillars on which slightly projecting springers rise from bases with simple torus mouldings. The transverse ribs of the nave are carried on dosserets. This arrangement for lightening the supports of the vault is most unusual.

The Cistercian tradition
Sankt Maria, Eberbach, before
1178–1186, plan. The nave is a long
vaulted basilican construction,
opening on to a projecting
transept. Each arm of the transept
carries three rectangular chapels.
The choir is narrower than the
nave and comprises a flat-ended
central apse. All this is typical of
the Cistercian tradition.

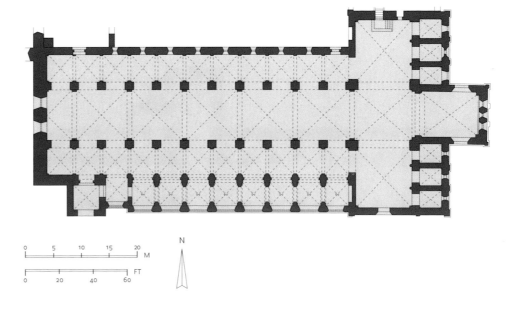

The British Isles

In 1066 William the Conqueror set out to claim the English throne promised to him by Edward the Confessor, defeating Harold II at the battle of Hastings. Harold was killed in the battle, and William was crowned King of England at Westminster, reigning from 1066 to 1087. The imposition of the feudal system followed, and with it came the spread of Norman Romanesque architecture.

This was a period of intense architectural activity. Fine buildings were constructed at Canterbury, Lincoln, Old Sarum, Rochester, Bury St Edmunds, St Albans, Winchester, Worcester, Gloucester, Norwich, Ely and Durham. From this period there have survived above all the nave of St Albans and the transept at Winchester. The buildings were mostly on a large scale, with long naves opening on to deep choirs. Rib vaulting made its appearance quite early. One of the characteristics of English Romanesque is the beauty of the towers, which were built at the façade, at the crossing, or at the entrance to the sanctuary. The most famous of these was the tower of St Albans, which dates from the mid-twelfth century. The tower at the crossing of Norwich cathedral imparts a monumental effect to the entire building. That of Bury St Edmunds (Suffolk) stood over the porch of the abbey, and has not survived. It was richly ornamented with arcades.

Durham cathedral, consecrated in 1133, is a fine example of Anglo-Norman architecture of the early twelfth century. It is the first English building to be rib-vaulted throughout. It has a nave and aisles, a widely projecting transept with east aisles, and a very deep choir, which ended in three apses, the axial apse being larger than the lateral ones (the apses have since been replaced by an east transept). The nave has a three-storey elevation: large arcades, wide quadrant-vaulted tribunes whose bays are divided by a central column, and a clerestory gallery.

The Norman influence is clear in the nave supports, where composite piers with engaged columns alternate with circular piers. It seems likely that this arrangement, which derives from Jumièges, was transmitted via Westminster and Ely. The supports are ill-adapted to carrying rib vaults. Moreover, the quarters of the rib vaults are infilled, whereas Gothic vaults are webbed. Nevertheless, these first experiments in vaulting led to the sexpartite and thus to the Gothic vault. In Normandy, as in England, there were numerous early experiments in vaulting, among them Gloucester, Lessay, Caen and the transept at Winchester. But timber-framed roofs were also used, as for example at Ely. There the nave is of twelve bays, with purely decorative alternation of supports, and the three storeys of the elevation are each accorded equal importance. The clerestory forms a tall, elegant portico. There is an extension at the west end in the form of a transept with a central tower, two smaller

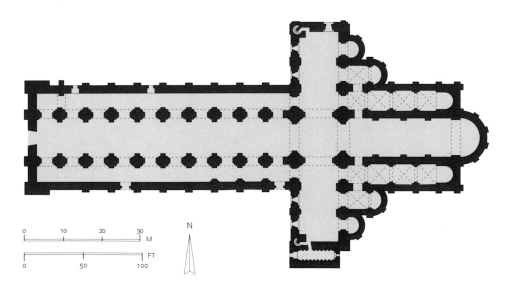

0 10 20 30
M
0 50 100
FT

N

Very early Romanesque
St Albans cathedral, before 1080, plan. The Romanesque building comprised a very wide nave, ten bays long, flanked by very narrow aisles. The strongly projecting transept had two oriented echelon chapels in each wing. The Romanesque choir presented a Benedictine plan with echelon chapels. Despite significant alterations, St Albans remains one of the oldest Romanesque buildings surviving in England.

An original Romanesque tower
St Albans cathedral, view from the south-west. The Gothic western parts, in white stone, contrast with the Romanesque eastern part, in brick, dominated by the crossing tower. This comprises a first level reinforced by flat buttresses and pierced with two semicircular bays. Above this are four double bays divided by colonnettes. The angle buttresses resemble cylindrical piers, and those at the centre of each face of the tower present two engaged columns.

Traces of painted decoration
St Albans cathedral, before 1080, nave wall. The bays are divided by wide, flat pilasters. The triple-moulded arcades are surmounted by vast bays opening on to the aisle roof-timbers. Above these is a clerestory with the usual Norman passage. The plaster that covers the brickwork has retained traces of painted decoration on the intrados and outer mouldings of the arcades: chevron, diamond and chequered designs are visible. The paintings on the piers are Gothic.

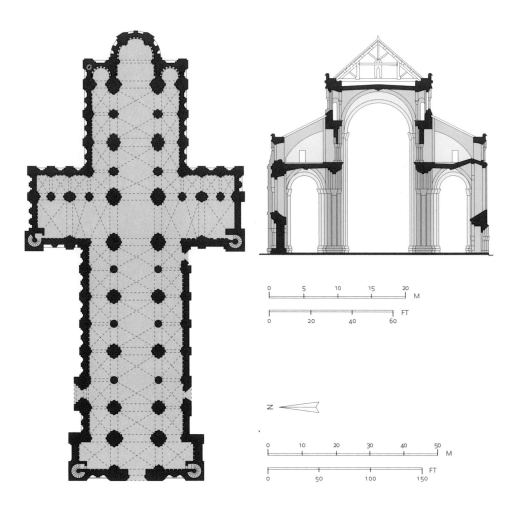

0 5 10 15 20 M

0 20 40 60 FT

N

0 10 20 30 40 50 M

0 50 100 150 FT

The long nave of English Romanesque
Durham cathedral, consecrated in 1133, plan and cross-section. The plan is a variant of the Benedictine formula, comprising a nave of four bays with single side aisles, a projecting transept with east aisles, and a deep, four-bay choir leading to a tripartite apse. The axial chapel projects; the other two are hollowed out of the flat wall of the chevet, in line with the aisles. Durham illustrates the new tendency in England towards longer churches with wider transepts.

Page 215
An ornate Romanesque interior
Durham cathedral. The three-storey elevation presents arcades, quadrant-vaulted tribunes with double bays and a clerestory with passage. The nave is divided from the aisles by powerful piers flanked by engaged semi-columns. The originality of the supports is their wealth of ornament: the heavy cylindrical piers are covered with incised diamonds, flutings and chevrons, which extend to the arches of the arcades and the vaulting ribs.

turrets and an oriented lateral apsidiole; this combines features of both the Carolingian westwork and the Romanesque innovations of the Empire.

Ely finds an echo in Norwich (1096– before 1145), where the nave of the cathedral is of similar elevation. But the peculiarity of Norwich is the east end. English Romanesque makes use of both the 'Benedictine' chevet with echelon chapels and the ambulatory with radiating chapels. The east end at Norwich is a sort of compromise between these styles. It has an ambulatory, but the central apsidiole was replaced in the thirteenth century by a large chapel and subsequently by a second chapel in 1430. The two lateral apsidioles, however, retain their original plan, as segments of two overlapping circles oriented parallel to the axis. The larger, west one serves as a chapel; the east one is a sanctuary. These very high apsidioles are decorated with blind arcades running the entire length of their outer walls. The choir is on three levels: arcades, tribunes with undivided bays, and a Gothic clerestory built after 1362. The elevation of the nave is similar. The clerestory has a low gallery opening on to the nave via arches. The nave exemplifies the tendency to elongation characteristic of English Romanesque; it has fourteen bays, and the choir has a further four.

The aspiration to lighten the wall-structure at tribune level and increase the number of galleries hollowed out of the walls is fully expressed in Peterborough cathedral. With the exception of the rib-vaulted aisles, the entire structure is timber-roofed. With the lateral thrust caused by stone vaulting thus eliminated, the three-storey elevation could be extended to every part of the building. The transepts thus received three storeys of windows, and there are narrow galleries at triforium and clerestory levels. These two passages extend round the entire perimeter of the building, and mark the fullest development of the thick Norman wall.

The most prestigious cathedral
Ely cathedral, first half of the twelfth century. The cathedral boasts a very long nave of twelve bays. The transept we see today is Romanesque, with the exception of the crossing tower, which collapsed in 1322. It was replaced by an octagonal lantern-tower of great daring and elegance. The exterior shows an ornamental exuberance that contrasts with the relative austerity of the interior.

Applied decoration on blind arcading
Ely cathedral, first half of the twelfth century, decoration of outside walls. The walls are divided into registers by moulded cordons. Bays with multiple archivolts, flanked by narrow blind niches, run between two rows of blind arcades, trefoil or semicircular, resting on colonnettes. The uprights of the jambs, the colonnettes of the window splays, the capitals and the archivolts are densely covered with plant motifs, figures, chevrons and diamonds. No space is left unadorned.

Exuberant ornament
Ely cathedral, mid-twelfth century. The surrounding mouldings of the bays and the masonry of the wall are decorated with chevrons that fold one into another.

During the twelfth century, and notably around 1130, a significant number of churches were built on the circular plan prevalent before the Conquest, though this time on a larger scale. Examples are at Clerkenwell, Little Maplestead and the Temple Church in London. The plan of the church of the Holy Sepulchre in Jerusalem, which had proved very popular in the West, was imitated in the rotunda of Saint Sepulchre at Cambridge; it has an annular ambulatory and raised central tower.

As early as the first half of the twelfth century, a four-storey elevation was attempted at Tewkesbury Abbey in Gloucestershire: arcade, tribune, triforium and clerestory. There was a new tendency to reduce the chevet to rectangular form. The spread of this formula was encouraged by the foundation of Cistercian monasteries. It can be seen at Southwell Minster and Romsey Abbey of around 1120, and then at Hereford, Llandaff, Southwark and Old Sarum. The Cistercian order was introduced into England at an early date; the monastery at Waverley was founded in 1128 at the behest of Giffard, Bishop of Winchester, and the monastery of Rievaulx was constructed in 1132 by the mother house of Clairvaux.

A luminous interior
Ely cathedral, mid-twelfth century, nave. The nave is timber-roofed and the side aisles are groin-vaulted. Above the arcade are high double bays and a clerestory in which the tall bays are each flanked by two narrow subsidiary bays. Cylindrical piers alternate with clustered engaged columns carrying cubic capitals. At the centre of each pier, semi-columns on dosserets rise from the floor to the wooden ceiling, ensuring a powerful vertical thrust.

A lengthy nave
Ely cathedral, plan. A deep porch, dating from the thirteenth century, opens into the west transept, of which only the south arm has survived. The nave is twelve bays long. The very wide east transept has east and west aisles, and opens on to a deep choir.

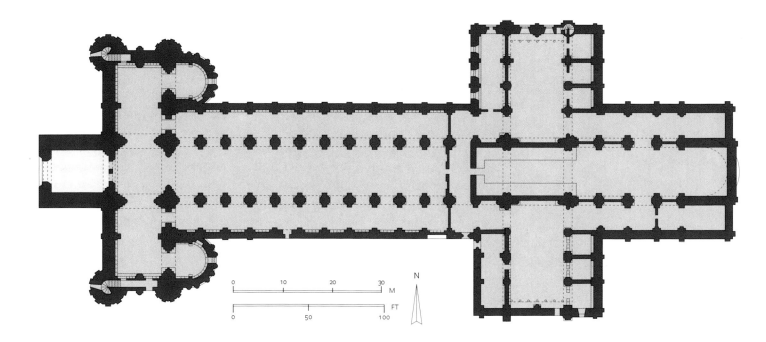

A four-level elevation

Ely cathedral, mid-twelfth century, interior. Above the slightly pointed arches of the arcade are three further levels: tribunes with triple arcades set between massive pillars, a narrow triforium, and a clerestory of wide semicircular bays. This four-level elevation was widely adopted in England.

Blind arcading

Ely cathedral, detail of internal ornament. The surface of the wall is covered with blind arcades of semicircular arches. These rest on simple cubic capitals and may intersect. The registers of arcades are emphasised by a row of chevrons. This relatively sober decorative scheme contrasts with the exuberance of the exterior.

A little later, in 1135, came Fountains Abbey in Yorkshire. It had single side-aisles, a projecting transept with four rectangular chapels and a choir with three rectangular echelon apses. The two-level elevation had slightly pointed arcades. The nave originally had a pointed barrel vault, which was replaced by a timber-framed roof. The aisles had a transversal pointed barrel vault. Fountains is now only a beautiful and evocative ruin, but was in its time the inspiration for many buildings in England and Ireland.

The final period of English Romanesque is illustrated by two buildings. The cathedral at Chichester (Sussex) has a Gothic-style nave and flying buttresses visible from the exterior, but conserved a three-storey elevation with clerestory. The external decoration at Ely cathedral consists of blind arcades so intricate as to resemble openwork. This style was taken up in Early English Gothic at Peterborough, Wells and Salisbury.

A painted ceiling

Peterborough cathedral, late twelfth century, crossing tower. The low central tower has twice been reconstructed, in circa 1315 and in the nineteenth century. The second reconstruction is a faithful copy of the Gothic tower of the early fourteenth century. The wooden ceiling extends from one end to the other; huge painted diamond shapes are picked out with painted mouldings.

Passages in upper storeys

Peterborough cathedral, interior from the transept. The transept dates from the late twelfth century. It has a single (west) aisle whose piers are alternately round and octagonal. The three-storey elevation continues in the arms of the transept, in the orthogonal bays of the choir and in the central section of the apse, where there is a timber roof. Passages are found in both intermediate and upper storeys, both of them running round the whole periphery of the building.

Page 220

An impressively homogeneous interior

Peterborough cathedral, late twelfth century, nave. The nave exhibits the classic Norman three-storey elevation. The arcades have numerous mouldings with occasional discreet chevron ornament. Projecting cordons separate the different levels. The double bays of the tribunes have a chevron moulding underlining the main arch. The high clerestory windows are flanked by two narrow bays that open only on to the passage running through the thickness of the wall. The painted wooden ceiling dates from the early years of the thirteenth century.

Page 222

A fortress tower
Tewkesbury Abbey, consecrated in 1121. Above a very plain square base with two windows in each side rises the three-storey tower with its slightly projecting turrets at each corner. The first storey has three bays under semicircular arcades; the second is lower, and presents narrow, blind intersecting arcades. The third is higher, and has two double bays in a frieze of blind arcades with chevron mouldings. Romanesque ornament also survives in the blind arcades of the transept arms and the continuous frieze of applied arcades at the top of the north wall of the nave.

Norman canons abandoned
Tewkesbury Abbey, nave. The nave has eight bays. The arcades occupy three-fifths of the total elevation, and rest on enormous cylindrical piers crowned with collar capitals. The triforium is very narrow and the clerestory windows are also small. This elevation constitutes a radical break with Norman practice, and suggests the aspiration towards a native English style.

The Romanesque Building Site

It is sometimes thought that the Romanesque building site lacked rational organisation. This is not the case. The status of the artist was already clearly recognised in society, as we know from the many surviving inscriptions by master masons, sculptors, mosaicists, painters and workers in precious metals. The organisation of work, the search for materials and their transport to the site, the planning of the site (particularly in relation to the different seasons of the year) and the sequence of building were all fully worked out.

Rather than listing proofs of this fact, I present a text from the last quarter of the twelfth century, in which Gervase of Canterbury describes the reconstruction of the choir of the cathedral, which had been destroyed by fire in 1174. It is one of the most complete and detailed texts that we have on twelfth-century preparation of materials and methods of construction. The document was written some time after 1184, and recounts the arrival of a French architect, Guillaume de Sens, who was made master of works between 1174 and 1178. The text also highlights the architectural controversy provoked by the transition from late Romanesque to early Gothic.

'After the fire, the monks opened the tombs of the saints and removed the sarcophagi from the ruined choir; they placed them in the nave and separated them from the congregation by a thin wall. The monks then sought advice on repairing the church. This phase lasted five years; the English and French architects consulted offered conflicting advice about reinforcing the pillars of the choir, which had been weakened by the fire. Eventually Guillaume de Sens was chosen as a man of excellent reputation and experienced in working with both wood and stone. The monks agreed to demolish the ruined choir. Guillaume designed ingenious machines for loading and unloading ships, and the stone was brought from France. He prepared models for the sculptors to use in their carvings, and made other preparations. In the first year, the choir was demolished. The following year, the pillars were erected row by row, and on these and on the external walls of the side-aisles arches and vaults were begun. The third year (1176–1177), two further pillars were constructed on either side, and the triforium and clerestory begun. The transept was started in 1178. But early in the fifth year, when the great vault was being built, the scaffolding collapsed from a height of fifty feet (15 m), injuring Guillaume de Sens so badly that he was forced to delegate the completion of the work to an intelligent and industrious monk.

In 1179, William the Englishman succeeded Guillaume de Sens. William was a short man, honest and clever. He completed both arms of the transept, joined the vault over the main altar, and prepared the foundations for enlargement of the church to the east with a new chapel devoted to Saint Thomas [à Becket]. While the foundations were being dug, William discovered the bodies of monks; these were transferred to a communal grave to the south. Then the crypt wall was built as far as the windows.

At the beginning of the sixth year, in 1180, when work began again after the winter, the monks wanted to inaugurate the building at Easter. The architect complied, accelerating the construction of the wall around the choir, within which three altars and various tombs were built. A wooden partition with three glazed windows was erected in the east part of the choir, in order to protect the unfinished interior from the elements.'

At this point, Gervase notes the differences between the old and new buildings, thus perfectly illustrating the architectural debate of the late twelfth century. 'The old pillars and the new were similar in form and diameter, but different in height. For the new structure, they were made some twelve feet (3.65 m) taller. In the old capitals, the carving was shallow, while the new ones exhibit fine sculptures. Around the choir, there were twenty-two pillars; now, there are twenty-eight. All the arches and all the forms of decoration were flat, since they were cut with a [stone-dressing] pick and not with a chisel. Now there are sculptures everywhere; before, there were no marble columns, and now there are very many. Around the choir, the vaults were flat; now they have ribs and vaults. Previously, a wall set on pillars separated the transept from the choir, now there is no longer a division; choir and transept seem to meet beneath a single boss, situated at the centre of the great vault, which rests on the four main ribs. Before, there were big paintings on the wooden ceiling, now the vault is stone-built. Before, there was a single triforium gallery; now there are two in the choir and a third in the nave of the church.'

From this privileged witness of the works at Canterbury, we learn that the Gothic building site was organised in the same way as the Romanesque, while architectural forms were gradually modified and adapted to the new taste. And this how we should think of the evolution of style, not as an abrupt transition but as a gradual process.

Left

Church building depicted

Vitae et passiones apostolorum. (Lives and Passions of the Apostles). Drawing in red and brown ink. A passage from the live of Matthew is illustrated here: 'The pious people built a church in thirty days'. The miniature shows different aspects of stone-cutting and building and gives special attention to the carving of capitals. (Bayerische Staatsbibliothek, Munich, Clm 13 074, fol. 90v)

Right

Romanesque illumination

Bible from Sant Pere de Rodes, late eleventh century, tempera on parchment. This bible was created by three artists. With the bibles of Ripoll and León, this one is among the most richly decorated manuscripts in Europe. (Bibliothèque Nationale, Paris, Ms. lat. 6,3; fol. 89v)

The work of the Romanesque sculptor

Gerona cathedral, second half of the twelfth century, detail of relief from cloister, showing two sculptors working on the different phases of smoothing the block of stone in preparation for the carving of a capital. We know that a sort of production line was used in the workshops where the capitals were carved. The sculptor worked in harness with the master mason and the stone-carvers. The Romanesque artist illustrated his work amid the sculpted decoration as a claim to recognition.

OUTLOOK

From Romanesque to Gothic

The origin of the Gothic style
Saint-Denis, Île-de-France, west façade, before 1140. The façade presents a central rose window, three portals and two lateral towers, and constitutes the first definitive achievement of the Gothic portal. Here column-statues have replaced the figures placed in the splays of the Norman portal; through their integration into the column the figures become part of the façade architecture.

The most important aspect of any study of Romanesque architecture is the part played by the various geographical and historical circumstances in the development of style. The architectural discoveries made during the Romanesque period were a precondition for the development of Gothic. The Romanesque architects of Normandy and England soon learnt to cover broad naves with a type of vaulting transmitted to the Gothic period: the intersecting rib vault. In order to span larger spaces, architects inserted a further rib passing through the boss and thus created the sexpartite vault. In the thirteenth century the square plan was replaced by an oblong, and transverse arches, which had previously been semicircular, were now pointed. In the fourteenth century the design of the vaults was complicated by the appearance of liernes connecting the boss to the point of the transverse rib, and of tiercerons joining the base of the transverse rib to the transverse ridge rib. Thereafter vaulting grew increasingly complex, and the vault was divided into many little panels by multiple ribs. The other essential component of Gothic architecture is the flying buttress, the origin of which is the abutment wall concealed in the roof structure of the side-aisles, serving to contain the thrust of the nave vaults.

The emphasis accorded to bell-towers during the Romanesque era was maintained, but they grew taller and more slender, in keeping with the prevailing tendency in Gothic to accentuate the vertical. The first Gothic architectural sculpture is found in the royal abbey of Saint-Denis; its west façade (before 1140) offers the first clear example of a Gothic portal, with statuary columns replacing the figures carved in the archivolts of the Romanesque doorway.

Whereas, in the north, Gothic quickly became established, with its rib vaults, statuary columns and ever-expanding areas of stained glass, Romanesque long remained the dominant style in the south and in Italy. The statues of Peter and Paul on the façade of Ripoll of about 1170–1180 are not reminiscent of the statuary columns of the Saint-Denis portal; the distinction is clear in the treatment of the slightly inclined head and of the halo, which hides the column. These figures are representational rather than structural in function. They exemplify the persistent Romanesque tendencies of the south at a time when Gothic had already conquered the north. The narthex of the abbey church at Vézelay and the royal portal at Chartres were both built during the third decade of the twelfth century. Distinctions of form rather than date (they were completed almost simultaneously) define the former as Romanesque, the latter as Gothic. This is particularly clear in the radically different place and function occupied by the religious imagery in each case.

CHRONOLOGICAL TABLE

Monuments

961	Gernrode: foundation of Sankt Cyriakus
989–1029	Orléans: Saint-Aignan
1022	Sant Pere de Rodes: consecration
1010–1033	Hildesheim: Sankt Michael
c. 1023	Mont-Saint-Michel: foundation of the Romanesque church
1025–1061	Speyer I
1025–1080	Limoges: Saint-Martial
1032/1034	Ripoll: consecration of Santa Maria
pre 1040	Saint-Michel-de-Cuxa: extension of the abbey built by Oliba
1040	Como: consecration of the cathedral Cardona: consecration of Sant Vicenç
1040–1067	Jumièges: Notre Dame

1045	Limburg an der Haardt: Benedictine abbey completed
1047	Périgueux: first abbey church of Saint-Front
pre 1049	Poitiers: construction of the bell-tower of Saint-Hilaire-le-Grand
1049	Ottmarsheim: consecration of Sankt Maria
1049	Reims: cathedral of Saint-Rémi completed
1050	Bernay: abbey church of Notre-Dame completed Vignory: consecration of the church of Saint-Étienne
1057	Leyre: consecration of San Salvador
c. 1059	Caen: foundation of the Abbaye-aux-Dames by Mathilda, wife of William the Conqueror; church of Sainte-Trinité begun

11th century   11th century

Events

Notre-Dame, Jumièges

987–996	Hugues Capet King of France: foundation of the Capetian dynasty
996–1002	Otto III German Emperor
996–1031	Robert the Pious King of France
1022	End of the episcopacy of Bernward of Hildesheim
1024–1032	Pontificate of John XIX
1029	Sancho III, King of Navarre, divides the kingdom into Aragon, Castile and Navarre
1031–1060	Henri I King of France
1032–1044	Pontificate of Benedict IX
1035–1065	Fernando I the Great King of Castile and León
1039–1056	Henry III German Emperor
1042–1066	Edward the Confessor, last Anglo-Saxon King of England before the Norman Conquest

1045–1046	Pontificate of Sylvester III
1045–1046	Pontificate of Gregory VI
1046–1047	Pontificate of Clement II
1047–1048	Second pontificate of Benedict IX
1048	Pontificate of Damasus II
1049–1054	Pontificate of Leo IX, beginnings of church reform
1055–1057	Pontificate of Victor II
1056–1106	Henry IV German Emperor
1057–1058	Pontificate of Stephen IX
1057–1059	Isaac I Comnenus Byzantine Emperor
1059	Robert Guiscard, Duke of Calabria and Apulia

Saint-Étienne, Vignory, false tribunes

Santiago de Compostela
cathedral, nave

1060 Conques: consecration of
Sainte-Foy
1060–1150 Toulouse: Saint-Sernin
1063 León: consecration of San Isidoro
1063–1094 Venice: remodelling of San Marco
1063–1100 Moissac: cloister of Saint-Pierre
c. 1063 Caen: foundation of the Abbaye-
aux-Hommes by William the
Bastard, later the Conqueror
1065 Cologne: consecration of Sankt
Maria im Kapitol
c. 1066 Frómista: monastery of San Martín
1067–1069 Cologne: Sankt Gereon
1067–1107 Silos: monastery of Santo Domingo
1068 Nevers: Saint-Étienne begun

1075–1080 Santiago de Compostela: cathedral
1076 Saint-Guilhem-le-Désert:
completion of the abbey
1077 St Albans begun
1077–1097 London: White Tower
1080–1106 Speyer II
1080–1130 Cluny III: abbey church (unfinished)

1081–1239 Mainz: cathedral
1093 Maria Laach: construction of the
abbey church begun
1093–1133 Durham: reconstruction of the
cathedral
1093–1190 Ely: construction of the cathedral
1094 San Juan de la Peña: consecration of
the monastery
1095 Como: consecration of
Sant'Abbondio
1096–1106 Vézelay: reconstruction of
Sainte-Madeleine
1096–1145 Norwich: cathedral
1098 Trani: construction of cathedral
begun
1099–1184 Modena: cathedral
before Loarre: castle of the
1100 Kings of Navarre
11th c. Loches: keep

11th century   11th century   11th century

1060–1091 Conquest of Sicily by the Normans
1060–1108 Philippe I King of France
1061–1073 Pontificate of Alexander II
1065 Alfonso I King of León
1066 Death of Edward the Confessor,
King of England
Battle of Hastings and Conquest
of England by William, Duke of
Normandy
1066–1087 Reign of William I the Conqueror,
King of England
1072 Normans capture Palermo

1072–1109 Reign of Alfonso VI of Castile and
León
1073 Death of Saint Domingo of Silos
1073–1085 Pontificate of Gregory VII:
Gregorian reform
1075–1085 Investiture Contest between Pope
Gregory VII and Emperor Henry IV
1076 Jerusalem captured by the Turks
1077 Emperor Henry IV humiliated
before Gregory VII at Canossa
1080 Death of Rudolf of Swabia at the
Battle of Merseburg

1081–1118 Alexius I Comnenus Byzantine
Emperor: Byzantine Empire reconstructed
1083 Sack of Rome by Robert Guiscard
1084 Henry IV crowned Emperor at Rome
by Antipope Clement III
1085 Capture of Toledo by Alfonso VI and
continued reconquest of Spain
1086–1087 Pontificate of Desiderius under the
name Victor III
1087–1100 Reign of William II of England
1088–1099 Pontificate of Urban II
1091 Pechenegs annihilated by Alexius I
Comnenus
1093 Pope Urban II returns to Rome
1095 Synod of Clermont: exhortation
to Crusaders
1096–1099 First Crusade
1097 Conflict between Alexius I
Comnenus and the Crusaders
1098 Cistercian order of monks founded
1099–1118 Pontificate of Paschal II

Sainte-Foy, Conques

Notre-Dame,
Paray-le-Monial

1100–1150 Clermont-Ferrand: Notre-Dame-du-Port
1106 Dijon: consecration of Saint-Bénigne
1107 Lyons: consecration of Saint-Martin-d'Ainay
1108 Southwell Minister begun
pre 1109 Paray-le-Monial: reconstruction of Notre-Dame
1110 Angoulême: construction of the cathedral of Saint-Pierre begun

1117–1138 Verona: reconstruction of San Zeno Maggiore
1118 Pisa: consecration of the unfinished cathedral
c. 1120 Houdan: keep begun
1120–1132 Autun: cathedral of Saint-Lazare
1120–1173 Périgueux: Saint-Front
after 1120 Vézelay: second campaign of Sainte-Madeleine
1123 Taüll: consecration of the churches of Sant Climent and Santa Maria
Tewkesbury: consecration of the abbey church
1123–1136 Rochester: royal castle
c. 1125 Saint-Martin-de-Boscherville: reconstruction of Saint-Georges completed

1130 Canterbury: consecration of the cathedral
1130–1140 Castle Hedingham: castle
1130–1145 Poitiers: Notre-Dame-la-Grande
pre 1131 La Seu d'Urgell: cathedral begun
1130–1144 Saint-Denis: Abbot Suger's basilica
1131–1180 La Seu d'Urgell: cathedral
1132 Pavia: consecration of San Pietro in Ciel d'Oro
1133 Clairvaux: construction of the abbey church of Clairvaux II begun
1133–1172 Hildesheim: Sankt Godehard
1135 Chiaravelle della Colomba: construction of abbey church begun
1139–1147 Fontenay: abbey church
1139–1187 Verona: cathedral

12th century | 12th century | 12th century

1100–1135 Henry I King of England
1102 Arrival of Almoravids in Spain
1104–1134 Reign of Alfonso I, King of Aragon and Navarre
1106 Henry I of England defeats his elder brother Robert
1106–1125 Reign of Henry V, German Emperor
1108–1137 Louis VI the Fat, King of France

1118–1143 Reign of John II Comnenus, Byzantine Emperor
1119–1124 Pontificate of Calixtus II
1121 Synod of Soissons, doctrines of Peter Abelard condemned
1122 Concordat of Worms, end of Investiture Contest
1122–1126 War between Byzantium and Venice
1122–1151 Abbacy of Suger at Saint-Denis
1124–1130 Pontificate of Honorius II
1125–1153 Abbacy of Saint Bernard at Clairvaux
1126–1157 Reign of Alfonso VII, King of Castile
1128 Marriage of Mathilda of England, daughter of Henry I, and Geoffrey Plantagenet, Count of Anjou

1130 Roger II de Hauteville, King of Sicily
Beginning of the schism of Anacletus II
1130–1143 Pontificate of Innocent II
1133 Imperial coronation of Lothair III
1135–1154 Reign of Stephen, King of England
1137 Marriage of Louis VII, King of France, and Eleanor of Aquitaine
Union of Aragon and Catalonia
1137–1180 Louis VII, King of France
1138 Conrad III of Hohenstaufen elected King of Germany
1139 Outbreak of civil war in England between Stephen and his cousin Mathilda

Tewkesbury cathedral

Fontenay abbey, cloister

1140/1143 Palermo: Palatine Chapel

c. 1140 Murano: Santi Maria e Donato completed

1147 Lucca: consecration of San Frediano

1148 Cîteaux: consecration of the abbey church of Notre-Dame

1149 Jerusalem: consecration of the church of the Holy Sepulchre

1150 Avallon: extension of the collegiate church of Saint-Lazare completed

c. 1150 Florence: construction of the baptistery and San Miniato al Monte Poitiers: Notre-Dame-la-Grande completed

1150–1250 Cologne: Gross Sankt Martin

1151 Schwarzrheindorf: consecration of double chapel of Sankt Klemens

1151–1174 Zamora: cathedral

1156–1191 Senlis: cathedral

Pisa cathedral

1155/1160– Laon: cathedral
1215–

1152 Pisa: construction of baptistery begun

1152–1200 Salamanca: Old Cathedral

c. 1160 Poblet: construction of the abbey church of Santa Maria begun

1162–1176 Coimbra: cathedral

pre 1171 Bari: reconstruction of San Nicola

1172–1177 Newcastle: royal castle

1174 Monreale: construction of cathedral begun

after 1174 Milan: Sant'Ambrogio

1175–1230 Soissons: cathedral

1176–1240 Wells: cathedral (first phase)

1177–1185 Avignon: Saint-Bénézet bridge

1178 Lessay: consecration of the abbey church of Sainte-Trinité

1179–1184 Canterbury: Trinity Chapel

1180–1190 Dover: castle

1182 Paris: cathedral of Notre-Dame

1185 Basle: reconstruction of the cathedral begun

after 1186 Chichester: reconstruction of the cathedral

1192 Lincoln: reconstruction of the cathedral begun

1194 Chartres: reconstruction of the cathedral begun

c. 1194 Gerona: 'Arabic baths'

1196 Parma: Baptistery

12th century   12th century   12th century

1141–1144 Conquest of Normandy by Geoffrey Plantagenet

1142–1181 Henry the Lion, Duke of Saxony and Bavaria

1144–1145 Pontificate of Lucius II

1145 Saint Bernard combats the Cathar heresy in the south of France

c. 1145 Beginning of Almohad conquest of Spain

1145–1153 Pontificate of Eugenius III

1146 Canonisation of Henry II, German Emperor

1147–1149 Second Crusade

1150 Repudiation of Eleanor of Aquitaine by Louis VII of France

1151 Death of Geoffrey Plantagenet

1152 Marriage of Henry Plantagenet, Count of Anjou and Duke of Normandy, and Eleanor of Aquitaine

1152–1190 Frederick I Barbarossa, German Emperor

1153 Death of Saint Bernard of Clairvaux

1153–1154 Pontificate of Anastasius IV

1154–1186 Pontificate of Adrian IV

1154–1189 Henry II of England, first Plantagenet king

1155 Frederick I Barbarossa crowned Emperor at Rome

1158–1214 Reign of Alfonso VIII, King of Castile

1159 Pontifical schism between Alexander III and Antipope Victor IV

1159–1181 Pontificate of Alexander III

1162–1196 Alfonso II the Chaste, King of Aragon

1167 Capture of Rome by Frederick I Barbarossa

1170 Assassination of Thomas à Becket, Archbishop of Canterbury

Zamora cathedral, interior view of the dome

1173 War between Louis VII of France and Henry II of England

1174 Peace of Montlouis between Henry II of England and his sons

c. 1176 Foundation of the Vaudois sect

1180–1223 Philippe Auguste, King of France

1181–1185 Pontificate of Lucius III

1181–1226 Saint Francis of Assis

1184 Condemnation of Vaudois sect

1185–1187 Pontificate of Urban III

1187 Pontificate of Gregory VIII

1187–1191 Pontificate of Clement III

1189 Death of William II of Sicily

1189–1192 Third Crusade

1189–1199 Richard I Lionheart, King of England

1191–1197 Henry VI, German Emperor

1191–1198 Pontificate of Celestine III

1194–1266 Hohenstaufen dynasty Kings of Sicily

1195 Death of Henry the Lion

1198 Imperial coronations of Philip I of Swabia and Otto IV of Brunswick

1198–1216 Pontificate of Innocent III

1199–1216 John, King of England

Glossary

Abbey: Community of monks or nuns led by an abbot or abbess.

Aisle: One of the secondary → naves that flank the central nave of a church.

Ambo: Elevated lectern used for reading the lesson.

Ambulatory: Semicircular gallery forming an extension of the → aisles; it encompasses the choir.

Antependium: (Latin *ante pendere*: hanging before) Originally, a veil or hanging in front of an altar. From the eighth century onwards often made of metal, sometimes of painted wood.

Apse: (Greek *hapsis*, Latin *absis* or *apsis*: circle, vault) Semicircular or polygonal interior space normally forming the east end of the church.

Apsidiole: Small → apse grafted on to the → ambulatory, the → transept, or the → aisles of a church.

Arcade: Open bay covered by an → arch supported by pillars or columns.

Arch: Architectural element that connects two supports separated by a space. The round arch offers a semicircular profile; the stilted arch is higher than it is wide; the segmental or raised arch wider than it is high; in the horseshoe arch, the curve continues beyond the semicircle; the ogee arch has two identical facing curves, each composed of two arcs, successively concave and convex; the polyfoil arch is made by the juxtaposition of many segments of a circle.

Architrave: Lowest part of an → entablature, resting directly on the → capitals of columns or other vertical supports.

Archivolt: Architrave mouldings or mouldings of an arch.

Ashlar: Squared stones with smooth faces laid in regular courses with fine joints.

Astragal: Moulded collar, semicircular in section, at the junction of a column and its → capital.

Atrium: Court surrounded by open galleries, situated in front of the church façade.

Aula: Large hall used as residence.

Baldaquin, baldacchino: A structure that symbolically protects the high altar or the baptismal font, composed of a covering usually supported by four small columns with capitals, connected by arches or → architraves.

Baptistery: (Latin *baptisterium*: bath or pool) The place where early Christians performed the rite of purification by water, or the sacrament of baptism. Starting in the sixth century, it became an independent building with no other purpose than the administration of baptism. It was generally of square, circular, or polygonal central plan, and stood adjacent to or near the church.

Base: The lowest element of a vertical support, generally composed of a carved element on a square or polygonal (uncarved) plinth.

Basilica: (Greek *basilike*: royal porch, then Latin *basilica*) In the Roman Empire, a rectangular edifice divided into a → nave and → aisles separated by rows of columns or pillars, terminated at one end by an apse; the whole covered by a timber roof. It served as a court of justice and a meeting hall. The Christian basilica presented the same basic plan, with a central nave higher than the aisles; the entrance was at one end, the apse or apses at the other. Normally the central apse was the same width as the nave.

Bastide: A settlement on a rectangular grid with a central square at the intersection of the two main axes.

Calefactory: In a monastery, the room with a fire to warm the old or infirm.

Canon: Cleric who follows the canons (laws) of the Church. Beginning in the Carolingian period, canons lived together in a religious community, near a → collegiate church or a → cathedral, and followed their own rule.

Capital: (Latin *caput*: head) Architectural element surmounting a column or other vertical support that receives the load from an → architrave or arch.

Cathedral: (Latin *cathedra*: chair, bishop's throne) Principal church of a → diocese and the primary place of worship in the Episcopal see.

Chancel: (Latin *cancellus*: railing) Railing or low enclosure usually composed of sculpted slabs and stone or marble pillars. Separates the space reserved for the clergy from the nave, where the congregation sits.

Chapter: 1. Canonical or monastic assembly at which a chapter of the Rule was read to begin the assembly. 2. A college of → canons serving a collegiate church or cathedral.

Chevet: The use of the term *chevet* in English is complicated by the fact that, in English Norman and subsequent architecture, a flat east end is usual. The term is therefore often limited to the → echelon apse scheme, with apse, ambulatory and radiating chapels. Moreover, orientation is more rigorously observed in English Romanesque architecture than elsewhere, so the alternative term 'east end' is uniquely appropriate to English architecture. Given the geographical range of this volume, the term 'chevet' has been used to describe the parts of a church east of the crossing without distinction of country or shape.

Chevron: Geometric decorative motif in the shape of a zigzag.

Choir: (Latin *chorus*) Liturgical section of a church reserved for the singers and clergy, usually at the east end. The choir is generally sited in the → chevet and sometimes includes a section of the nave. The word is also applied to the space to the west reserved for singers.

Ciborium: (Latin from Greek, a cup) In Christian architecture, a light construction carried on slender columns and connected by architraves or arches that symbolically protects the high altar or the baptismal font.

Cimborio: A type of → dome specific to Spanish Romanesque.

Clerestory: The range of windows high up in the → nave, above the roof line of the side-aisles and therefore allowing light directly into the nave.

Cloister: (Latin *claustrum*, *claudere*: to close) Court or courtyard, often square or rectangular, bordered by an open colonnade, reserved for monks or nuns and surrounded by the buildings central to monastic life.

Collegiate church: A church, generally surrounded by monastic buildings, run by a → chapter of canons.

Column: Vertical architectural support composed of a shaft supported on a base and crowned by a → capital.

Confessio: (Latin *confessio*: public declaration) The place where the body of a martyr (or, later, of a confessor) was deposited. By extension, the sepulchral → vault under the sanctuary of a church that contains the tomb of a saint.

Consecration: Rite that sanctifies a place of worship by dedicating it to God.

Council: (Latin *concilium*) Assembly of bishops who establish texts and canons and issue decrees on problems of doctrine and ecclesiastical discipline.

Crossing: The part of a church at the end of the nave, between the arms of the transept, and west of the → chevet.

Crypt: (Latin *crypta*: subterranean gallery, burial vault) Vaulted space generally under a church, usually under the → choir. Often holds tombs.

Diocese: (Greek, then Latin *dioecesis*) Beginning in the fourth century, an administrative district comprising several parishes; later, an ecclesiastical district under the control of the bishop, which often corresponded to the territory of an ancient city.

Dome: A hemispherical → vault covering part of a church. Often synonymous with cupola.

Dosseret: Block placed above capital and below the spandrel of an → arch.

Echelon apse: Arrangement of east end by which the successively lower levels of the → transept, → choir and → ambulatory and radiating chapels form a harmonious whole.

Entablature: Horizontal crowning of an architectural order comprising a cornice, a frieze and an → architrave.

Extrados: Upper, outer curved face of a → vault or an arch or, sometimes, of a lintel course or → lintel.

Galilee: Entrance porch or chapel of a church.

Garth: Space enclosed by the arcades of a → cloister.

Guilloche: Ornament of → interlacing bands.

Historiated: Carved with a narrative sequence.

Impost: The upper part of a pillar supporting an arch.

Interlace: Decorative motif created from intertwined lines imitating braids or basketwork.

Intrados: Lower, inner face of a → vault or arch, also called a soffit.

Jacquet: (French) Pilgrim to Santiago de Compostela.

Keystone: (Latin *clavis*: key) Wedge-shaped stone in a lintel, vault, or arch.

Lierne: Short rib rising from transverse rib to boss.

Lintel: Horizontal member in wood or stone supporting the masonry above a door or window.

Lombard band: The series of blind → arcades, normally just under the cornice, forming a corbel-table. A characteristic Romanesque ornament.

Martyrium: Building marking the site of the martyrdom or tomb of a martyr. By extension, a commemorative funerary edifice, generally square, polygonal, or semicircular in plan.

Metope: Space between triglyphs above the → architrave of an → entablature.

Monastery: (Latin *monasterium*) Group of buildings intended to accommodate a community of monks or nuns.

Motte: Original form of the medieval castle. An artificial mound of earth was crowned with a wooden keep surrounded by a palisade and a moat. A sloping ramp gave access to the upper part, while a fixed bridge allowed access from the motte to the bailey below. The bailey contained buildings dependent on the castle, such as houses and a chapel. It was surrounded by a further palisade and moat.

Narthex: Used here in the sense of antechurch: a porch of two or more storeys, sometimes with a chapel in the upper section, sometimes framed by towers.

Nave: In a rectangular church, the central space between the front façade and the entrance to the apse or the crossing.

Pendentive: Small supporting → vault which facilitates a change in the plan on any level of the construction.

Pilaster: Rectangular, usually shallow vertical support placed against a wall or let into the wall, sometimes having a base and a capital.

Pilaster-strip: A pilaster, normally without structural function; series of pilaster-strips formed an external mural decoration characteristic of Romanesque architecture. Where the pilaster-strips are topped with shallow blind arcades, the latter are called a → Lombard band or corbel-table.

Pillar: Rectangular, polygonal or circular vertical support.

Plan: Representation of a construction showing a horizontal section at floor level.

Plat band: Flat horizontal moulding.

Polyfoil window: A window with several lobes: for example, trefoil (three lobes).

Portico: (Latin *porticus*) Colonnaded space, usually forming a porch, that opens on to the outside, located on the ground floor or the first floor and supported by → columns.

Relics: The bodily remains of a saint or clothing and objects associated with him or her.

Reliquary: Chest holding the relics of a saint that can be displayed to the faithful. During the Middle Ages, a small reliquary in the shape of a sarcophagus or church was known as a *châsse*.

Rotunda: Circular-plan edifice, usually covered with a timber roof or a → dome.

Salomonic column: A twisted barley-sugar column.

Sanctuary: Section of a church reserved for the clergy that contains the altar and where the liturgy is performed.

Sauveté: Township founded by a monastery as a sanctuary for fugitives.

Spolia: Stones, columns and other parts of classical buildings re-used in later architecture.

Squinch: An arch (or series of arches) at the corner of a square. Squinches make the transition between a square plan and a circular → dome.

Stylobate: Masonry base on which a colonnade rests.

Synod: Meeting of the priests and bishops of a province, convened by the archbishop.

Talus: Inclined bank at base of castle wall.

Tierceron: Short rib in rib → vault running from transverse rib to transverse rib ridge.

Transept: Transverse part of a church that intersects the longitudinal body of the edifice at a right angle and separates the → chevet from the nave. The arms are the two parts of the transept that extend from either side of the crossing; these are often of the same width as the nave and aisles.

Translation of relics: Liturgical displacement of relics from one place to another. This transfer often accompanies the dedication of a church.

Tribune: Gallery extending over the full width of a side-aisle, giving on to the nave through bays and on to the outside through windows.

Triforium: Narrow gallery between the ground arcades and the → clerestory, opening on to the nave through bays.

Trumeau: Central pillar supporting the → lintel and dividing a portal in two.

Tympanum: Semicircular space above the → lintel, monolithic or bonded, in which large-scale compositions could be sculpted.

Vault: Masonry structure that covers a space between two lateral walls and that presents an → intrados and an → extrados. The barrel vault is of semicircular form, like a half-cylinder, though later forms are slightly pointed; the groin vault is formed by the right-angled intersection of two barrel vaults; the rib vault is a groin vault carried on diagonal ribs. The ribs divide the rib vault into a number of webs, and it is thus described as quadripartite (four webs), sexpartite (six webs) and so on.

Voussoir: Wedge-shaped stones in arches and vaults on both the → intrados and → extrados, a series of which forms the inside face of an arch or vault.

Westwork: (German *Westwerk*) Group of architectural structures placed at the west end of a church, generally at the entrance, which may include several storeys, one or more towers, a porch, a high gallery with a chapel, the first bays of the nave, and sometimes a counter-choir.

Bibliography

Abou-el-Hadj, B.: 'Bury St. Edmunds Abbey between 1070 and 1124: a history of property, privilege and monastic art Production', in: *Art History*, VI, 1983.

Alexander, J. J. G.: *Medieval Illuminators and their Methods of Work*, Yale, 1992.

Aubert, M.: 'La construction au Moyen-Âge', in: *Bulletin Monumental*, 1960, pp. 241–259; 1961, pp. 7–42, 81–120, 181–209, 297–323.

Bango Torviso, I,: *El románico en España*, Madrid, 1992.

Barber, M.: *The Town Cities. Medieval Europe 1050–1320*, London, 1992.

Barral i Altet, X., Avril, F. and D. Gaborit-Chopin: *Le monde roman 1060–1220*. 2 vols., Paris, 1982 and 1983 (=L'Univers des formes).

Barral i Altet, X.: *La catedral romànica de Vic*, Barcelona, 1979 (= Art romànic, 7).

Barral i Altet, X.: *Artistes, artisans et production artistique au Moyen-Âge*, 3 vols, Paris, 1986–1989.

Barral i Altet, X.: *Le Paysage monumental de la France autour de l'an mil*, Paris, 1987.

Barral i Altet, X.: *Compostelle. Le grand chemin*. Paris, 1993 (=Découvertes).

Barral i Altet, X.: L'art préroman et l'art roman, in: *L'Art espagnol*, Paris, 1996, pp. 83–143.

Baylé, M.: *L'Architecture normande au Moyen-Âge*, Caen, 1996.

Bernward von Hildesheim und das Zeitalter der Ottonen, Exhibition catalogue, 2 vols, Hildesheim, 1993.

Biddle, M.: 'The development of the Anglo-Saxon towns', in: *S. S. Spoleto*, v. XXI (1), 1973, pp. 203–232.

Bony, J.: Durham et la tradition saxonne, in: *Études d'art médiéval offertes à Louis Grodecki*, Paris, 1981, pp. 79–92.

Braunfels, W.: *Abendländische Klosterbaukunst*, Cologne, 1969.

Cabañero Subiza, B.: *Los castillos catalanes del siglo X*, Saragossa, 1996.

Caillet, J. P.: *L'Art du Moyen-Âge*, Paris, 1995.

Chastel, A.: *L'Art italien*, Paris, 1995.

Chelini, J. and Branthôme, H.: *Les chemins de Dieu, Histoire des pelerinages Chrétiens des origines à nos jours*, Paris, 1982.

Clanchy, M. T.: *From Memory to Written Record: England 1066–1307*, 2nd ed., London, 1993.

Cluny III, La maior ecclesia, Exhibition catalogue, Musée Ochier, Cluny, 1988.

Conant, K. J.: *Cluny: les églises et la maison du chef d'ordre*, Mâcon, 1968.

Conant, K. J.: *Carolingian and Romanesque Architecture, 800–1200*, 2nd ed., Harmondsworth, 1978.

Courtens, A.: *Belgique romane*, Paris, 1969.

Crozet, R.: *L'Art roman en Berry*, Paris, 1932.

Crozet, R.: *L'Art roman en Poitou*, Paris, 1948.

Crozet, R.: *L'Art roman en Saintonge*, Paris, 1971.

Das Reich der Salier 1024–1125, Exhibition catalogue, Speyer, 1992.

Decker, H.: *L'Art roman en Italie*, Paris, 1958.

Dehio, G. and G. von Bezold: *Die kirchliche Baukunst des Abendlandes*, 2 vols of text, 5 vols of plates, Stuttgart, 1884–1901.

Die Zeit der Staufer. Geschichte – Kunst – Kultur, Exhibition catalogue, 5 vols, Stuttgart, 1977.

d'Onofrio, M.: *Les Normands, peuple d'Europe 1030–1200*, Paris, 1994.

Dubourg-Noves, P.: 'Des mausolées antiques aux cimborios romans d'Espagne. Évolution d'une forme architecturale', in: *Cahiers de Civilisation médiévale*, XXIII, 1980, pp. 323–360.

Duby, G.: *Saint Bernard, l'art cistercien*, Paris, 1976.

Duby, G.: *L'Europe au Moyen-Âge*, Paris, 1981, new ed. 1990.

Early Medieval Art in Spain, Exhibition catalogue, New York, 1993.

English Romanesque Art 1066–1200, Exhibition catalogue, London, 1984.

Erlande-Brandenburg, J.: *La Cathédrale*, Paris, 1990.

Esquieu, Y.: *Autour de nos cathédrales. Quartiers canoniaux du sillon rhodanien et du littoral méditerranéen*, Paris, 1992.

Europalia 85 España, Santiago de Compostela, 1000 ans de Pèlerinage Européen, Centrum voor Kunst en Cultuur, Abbaye Saint-Pierre, Ghent, 1985.

Fergusson, P.: *Architecture of Solitude: Cistercian Abbeys in Twelfth-Century England*, Princeton, 1984.

Focillon, H.: *L'Art d'Occident. Le Moyen-Âge roman et gothique*, Paris, 1938, new ed. 1965.

Focillon, H.: *L'An mil*, Paris, 1952.

Fournier, G.: *Le château dans la France médiévale. Essai de sociologie monumentale*, Paris, 1978.

Francastel, P.: *L'Humanisme roman. Critique des théories sur l'art du XIe siècle en France*, 1942, new ed. 1970.

Galicia no tempo, Exhibition catalogue, Monasterio de San Martino Pinario, Santiago de Compostela, 1983.

Garrigou Grandchamp, P.: *Demeures médiévales. Cœur de la cité*, Paris, 1992.

Grand, R.: *L'Art roman en Bretagne*, Paris, 1958.

Grodecki, L.: *Au seuil de l'art roman. L'architecture ottonienne*, Paris, 1958.

Grodecki, L., F. Mütherich, J. Taralon, F. Wormald: *Le siècle de l'An mil (950–1050)*, Paris, 1973, (= L'Univers des formes).

Guida del peregrino medieval (codex Calixtinus), Sahagún, 1990.

Gybal, A.: *L'Auvergne, berceau de l'art roman*, Clermont-Ferrand, 1957.

Harvey, J. H.: *The Medieval Architect*, London, 1972.

Heck, C.: *Moyen-Âge. Chrétienté et Islam*, Paris, 1996.

Heers, J.: *La ville au Moyen-Âge en Occident. Paysages, pouvoirs et conflits*, Paris, 1990.

Heinrich der Löwe und seine Zeit. Herrschaft und Repräsentation der Welfen 1125–1235, Exhibition catalogue, 3 vols, Brunswick, 1995.

Héliot, P.: 'Les origines du donjon résidentiel et les donjons-palais romans de France et d'Angleterre', in: *Cahiers de Civilisation médiévale*, 1974, pp. 217–234.

Kubach, H. E.: *Romanesque Architecture*, London, 1988.

Kubach, H. E. and H. Verbeek: *Romanische Kirchen an Rhein und Maas*, Cologne, 1972.

La Façade romane, International Conference, Poitiers, 1990, in: Cahiers de civilisation médiévale, XXXIV, 1991.

Lassale, V.: *L'influence antique dans l'art roman provençal*, Paris, 1970.

Le Goff, J.: *La civilisation de l'Occident médiéval*, Paris, 1984.

Les Normands, peuple d'Europe, 1030–1200, Exhibition catalogue, Venice, Caen, Toulouse, 1994–1995.

Lesueur, Dr. F.: Saint-Martin de Tours et les origines de l'art roman, in: *Bulletin Monumental*, 1949, pp. 7–84.

Mallet, J.: *L'Art roman de l'ancien Anjou*, Paris, 1984.

Mengozzi, O.: *La città italiana nell'alto Medioevo*, Florence, 1931.

Mesqui, J.: *Château et Enceintes de la France médiévale. De la défense à la résidence*, 2 vols, Paris, 1991 and 1993.

Norton, C.: *Cistercian Art and Architecture in the British Isles*, Cambridge, 1986.

Ornamenta Ecclesiae. Kunst und Künstler der Romanik, Exhibition catalogue, 3 vols., Cologne, 1985.

Ottaway, J.: 'Traditions architecturales dans le nord de la France pendant le premier millénaire', in: *Cahiers de civilisation médiévale*, 1980, pp. 141–172 and 221–239.

Pacaut, M.: *Les ordres monastiques et religieux au Moyen-Âge*, Paris, 1970.

Poly, J. P. and E. Bournazel: *La mutation féodale, Xe–XIIe siècle*, Paris, 1980.

Prache, A.: *Île-de-France romane*, La Pierre-qui-vire, 1983.

INDEX – Places

Pressouyre, L.: *Le rêve cistercien*, Paris, 1991.

Puig i Cadafalch, J.: *Le Premier Art roman. L'architecture en Catalogne et dans l'Occident méditerranéen aux Xᵉ et XIᵉ siècles*, Paris, 1928.

Puig i Cadafalch, J.: *La géographie et les origines du premier art roman*, Paris, 1935.

Reinhardt, H.: 'Les églises de Champagne après l'an mil', in: *Cahiers de civilisation médiévale*, 1961, pp. 149–158.

Rhein und Maas: Kunst und Kultur 800–1400, Exhibition catalogue, 2 vols, Cologne and Brussels, 1972.

Roux, S.: *Le Monde des villes au Moyen-Âge, Xᵉ–XVᵉ siècle*, Paris, 1994.

Saint Bernard et le monde cistercien, Paris, 1990–1991.

Saint-Sernin de Toulouse, trésors et métamorphoses, deux siècles de restaurations 1802–1989, Exhibition catalogue, Musée Saint-Raymond, Toulouse, 1989–1990.

Salmi, M.: *L'Art italien*, Florence, 1953.

Sapin, C.: *La Bourgogne préromane*, Paris, 1986.

Sauerländer, W. and J. Henriet: *Le siècle des cathédrales. 1140–1260*, Paris, 1989.

The Golden Age of Anglo-Saxon Art, 966–1066, Exhibition catalogue, London, 1984.

Vallery-Radot, J.: *Églises romanes. Filiations et échanges d'influences*, Paris, 1931.

Venturi, A.: *Storia dell'arte italiana*, Milan, 1904.

Vergnolle, E.: *L'Art roman en France. Architecture, sculpture, peinture*, Paris, 1994.

Viollet-le-Duc, E.: *Essai sur l'architecture militaire au Moyen-Âge*, Paris, 1854.

White, J.: *Art and Architecture in Italy 1250 to 1400*, Harmondsworth, 1966.

Yarwood, D.: *The Architecture of Italy*, London, 1970.

Yarza, J.: *Arte y arquitectura en España, 500–1200*, Madrid, 1979.

Index – Persons

Acknowledgements and Credits

The author would like to thank Sophie le Pennec for the scientific coordination and Caroline Keller for the editorial care of this publication.
The majority of the photographs illustrating this book have been taken by Claude Huber.
Numerous photographs are from Anne and Henri Stierlin: Pages 6, 11, 22, 23, 25, 26, 27, 28, 29, 31, 32–33, 45, 52, 55, 56, 57 above, 61, 63, 64, 65, 66, 67 left above and right, 69, 70, 71, 73, 74, 75, 77, 78, 79 above left, above right and below, 81, 85, 86, 87, 88–89, 89 above, 92, 99, 100, 105, 106, 107, 110, 112, 113, 115, 116, 119, 127 below, 139, 140, 140–141, 142, 143, 144, 145, 146, 147, 148, 149, 150, 154, 156, 157, 158, 159, 160, 161, 162, 163, 164, 165, 166, 167, 168, 169, 170 left and right, 171 above left and right, 178 right, 187 and 188.
The following documents are from the author's own archives: Pages 5, 30 above, 51, 67 below left, 171 below and 225 below.
In addition, a series of documents were helpfully provided by various institutions and photographers, in particular:
Pages 3 and 47 left: © Dom-Museum Hildesheim (Frank Tomio)
Page 9: © Parish Sankt Kunibert
Page 12: © RMN – H. Lewandowski
Pages 30 bottom, 199, 200 and 211: © Florian Monheim
Page 82: © Peter Willi
Pages 90, 182 and 183 left: © André Corboz
Page 91: © Georg Gerster
Page 183 right: © Zodiaque
Pages 184 and 186: © Scala
Page 195: © Westfälisches Landesmuseum für Kunst und Kulturgeschichte Münster, loan from private property
Pages 209 and 210: © Celia Körber-Leupold
Page 225 above left: © Bayerische Staatsbibliothek, Munich
Page 225 above right: © Cliché Bibliothèque nationale de France, Paris
Page 226: © Gérard Monico
Finally, the plans were created especially for this book by Alberto Berengo Gardin: Pages 8, 9, 20, 22, 26, 31, 36, 49, 54, 62, 66, 68, 72, 84, 88, 97, 98, 104, 106, 108, 111, 118, 120, 129, 136, 138, 161, 165, 172, 173, 175, 180, 190, 198, 199, 205, 206, 208, 211, 212, 214 and 218.